MW01070462

Also available in **BIG** print

for the visually impaired.

Our FIGHT

Survive and Thrive

In Spiritual Warfare

Pastor Zach Terry

2 Corinthians 10: 4

4 For the weapons of our warfare are not of the flesh but have divine power to destroy strongholds.*

*All scripture quoted will be in the English Standard Version unless otherwise noted.

"The words fall with power on the heart of even the average child of God because they are the words of the one who created us for more. "Come and follow me," the call comes more distinctly. The heart beats faster, stirred by a yearning that has awakened from long slumber."

Zach Terry

Dedication

To Evangelist Sam Cathy, who did for me what Elisha did for his servant; opened my eyes to a world unseen.

Credits

Cover Graphic by Zach Terry

Annie Keys, contributing editor

Table of Contents

We Want To See Jesus

We want to see Jesus,

To reach out and touch Him,

And say that we love Him.

Open our ears, Lord,

And help us to listen,

Open our eyes, Lord,

We want to see Jesus.

Open our hearts, Lord,

That we might receive You,

Open our spirits,

and teach us to worship.

Open our lips, Lord,

and teach us to praise You,

Open our eyes, Lord,

We want to see Jesus.

By Robert Cure

©Maranatha Music 1976

Chapter 1

The End of Status Quo

Anyone who makes a distinct effort to Biblically expose Satan and his hordes of demons for their true selves has learned that you enter this subject at your own risk. When I first taught this material at the church where I served as Senior Pastor, it was the genesis of some of the most challenging days I had faced up to that point.

During the next year, twenty percent of our congregation left the church for various reasons. Over one hundred people gone; some left over theological disagreements. Others left because of stylistic choices in our worship. With that in mind, also understand that the hand of God was working so mightily that our attendance never dropped.

The Lord brought so many new people and so many souls were saved that we actually held our own that year. We realized record numbers in attendance and baptized more during that time than at any time in the history of the Church.

We came through the storm ready to claim new ground for our Lord, Jesus Christ. The people recognized that Satan had tipped his hand. The combination of disgruntled members, exposed sin and infighting were not merely by chance; we were under demonic attack. Studying the tendencies of the enemy brought me great joy in the midst of the battle. I realized we must be doing something that irritated him terribly.

The great Protestant pastor, C. H. Spurgeon (1834-1892) once said, "Satan never kicks a dead horse." I would add that he doesn't attack dead churches, he coddles them. He softly sings a lullaby through the weak worship and anemic preaching.

The great southern revivalist, Vance Havner (1901-1986) said, "The Church in America is operating so far below the scriptural norm that if they were to rise to the level of normal the whole world would think they were fanatics."

Satan cannot steal the souls of God's elect so his efforts are given completely to disarming, hushing and tucking them into their nice warm beds of complacency. Only when the sleeping Christian attempts to rise to their feet, take up their sword and engage the enemy on behalf of themselves, their family and their Church, that demons will pull out their entire arsenal.

With ridicule, contempt, gossip, slander, temptation, sickness and discouragement, Satan's minions make a valiant effort to pull the waking warrior back into the ranks of complacency. Too often the attacks are successful and a person's journey to missional effectiveness is cut short.

The brave soldier falls back into the ranks of mundane church membership and returns to their previous state of slumber. However, occasionally, a person hears a distant voice. It is faint but unmistakable, "Come and follow me," it whispers.

The words fall with power on the heart of even the average child of God because they are the words of the one who created us for more. "Come and follow me," the call comes more distinctly. The heart beats faster, stirred by a yearning that has awakened from long slumber.

A passionate choice is made and the chains fall off! The crowd of the common calls out in discouragement and complacency because they haven't yet heard the voice. Yet, the true warrior marches on.

The extraordinary soldier fixes his attention so fiercely on the voice of He who is calling that the screaming masses grow silent. He can think of nothing else but spiritual progress and the growing Kingdom reign of Jesus Christ; the one who called.

Here's the deal, the status quo is comfortable. As a matter of fact, it is very comfortable. Most people have chosen the comfort of mediocrity and will never reach their God given potential. I choose to believe that you are different or you would not be reading this book.

You do not want to stand in eternity gazing back at a life that was wasted sleeping with the enemy. What is the solution; spiritual contact lenses.

Chapter 2
Spiritual Contact Lenses

I remember sitting on the second row of my Church as a child trying, straining to read the large Church covenant hanging on the wall about fifteen feet in front of me. From my perspective, it was all one big blur.

The bad thing about growing up with poor vision is you are not aware of it. You do not realize how much is actually going on in the world around you. You think that everyone around you has the same perspective as you do.

My first realization that something wasn't right was after my fifteenth birthday when I applied for my driver's learning permit. The person conducting the test told me I'd passed in all areas except one; I'd failed the vision test.

They suggested that I have my vision tested. At the Optometrist, I found out I was very near sighted and was fitted with a trial pair of contact lenses. I will never forget walking out of the Optometrist office wearing my contact lenses for the first time.

I was amazed to see thousands of leaves on an old oak tree, individually. The clarity of road signs and billboards was startling; it was as if an entire world that I'd never seen before, jumped into existence.

For many of us, this is an accurate analogy of our experience with the spirit world. We need God to provide clarity, spiritual lenses through which we can clearly perceive and analyze the world around us. God's answer to our spiritual near sightedness is His Word.

The purpose of this book is to guide you through scripture as it provides you with the spiritual contact lenses you need to see what was there all along. No doubt, some of the things you read will be just as shocking to you as the new world I found outside the Optometrist's office.

With time, you will gain your equilibrium and learn to function productively in this new world. Now, sit back in your chair and let's get you fitted with your pair of spiritual contact lenses.

<u>The Story of Balaam</u>   According to scripture there is an entire race of spirit beings inhabiting our world which cannot be seen by fallen humanity without divine enablement.

Missiologist Paul Heibert points out that American's are uniquely blind to the reality of this third dimension of spiritual life in what he called the, "Flaw of the excluded middle."

Throughout most of the world a theology of spirit beings, whether they are called angels, demons, ghosts, devils, fairies, or gnomes, is normative. God's Word gives clear direction to those who face these very distinct realities. Numbers Twenty two records the story of a man who made himself a prophet for profit.

By the time the name, "Balaam," appears in the scripture, the children of Israel have finished their wanderings in the wilderness and are encamped in the plains of Moab near the Jordan, ready to lay claim to the land promised to them by God.

Balak, the King of Moab, recognized the threat that Israel posed and determined to use all the weapons at his disposal to defend his city. According to the scriptures, Balak sent messengers to an enigmatic character named Balaam.

Exactly who Balaam was or why he seemed to be remarkably gifted by God remains a mystery. It does seem, however, that Balaam could prophecy over a people or circumstance and it would happen just as he said. The definition of "prophesy" is "to utter under divine inspiration." Apparently, Balaam had this gift.

Balak thought Balaam held the potential of hope for Moab, so he sent messengers with bribe money asking Balaam to speak against Israel. Balaam should have recognized God's favor on Israel and refused Balak's request outright. But, instead, Balaam inquired of the Lord for permission to curse God's chosen people.

The answer was a resounding, "No." King Balak, however, was too crafty to take, "No" for an answer. Again, he sent more distinguished messengers begging Balaam for assistance. This time he promised great wealth to Balaam; making him an offer he could not refuse.

Again Balaam approached God for permission to entertain Balak's request. It is at this point that God seems to be greatly offended by Balaam's repeated request. Apparently, God told Balaam to go to Balak, but later in the narrative, we will see that God rebukes him for going.

I think Matthew Henry was correct when he wrote, "It was in anger that God said to Balaam, 'Go with them,' and we have reason to think that Balaam himself so understood it, for we do not find him pleading this allowance when God reproved him for going." Then, the story takes an interesting turn that gives us some insight into the invisible spiritual world around us.

Numbers 22:22- (NASB)

The Angel and Balaam

22 But God was angry because he was going, and the angel of the LORD took his stand in the way as an adversary against him. Now he was riding on his donkey and his two servants were with him.

23 When the donkey saw the angel of the LORD standing in the way with his drawn sword in his hand, the donkey turned off from the way and went into the field; but Balaam struck the donkey to turn her back into the way.

24 Then the angel of the LORD stood in a narrow path of the vineyards, with a wall on this side and a wall on that side. 25 When the donkey saw the angel of the LORD, she pressed herself to the wall and pressed Balaam's foot against the wall, so he struck her again.

26 The angel of the LORD went further, and stood in a narrow place where there was no way to turn to the right hand or the left. 27 When the donkey saw the angel of the LORD, she lay down under Balaam; so Balaam was angry and struck the donkey with his stick.

28 And the LORD opened the mouth of the donkey, and she said to Balaam, "What have I done to you, that you have struck me these three times?" 29 Then Balaam said to the donkey, "Because you have made a mockery of me! If there had been a sword in my hand, I would have killed you by now."

30 The donkey said to Balaam, "Am I not your donkey on which you have ridden all your life to this day? Have I ever been accustomed to do so to you?" And he said, "No."

31 Then the LORD opened the eyes of Balaam, and he saw the angel of the LORD standing in the way with his drawn sword in his hand; and he bowed all the way to the ground.

****

It was at that point in verse 31 that, "Then the LORD opened the eyes of Balaam, and he saw the angel of the LORD standing in the way with his drawn sword in his hand; and he bowed all the way to the ground."

Was the angel there all along? Yes! Why could Balaam not see the Angel while the animal he rode upon could? The text doesn't tell us, but the reality of this event gives us one occasion when a human interacted with a spiritual being without being aware of it. This was one of God's Holy Angels!

Balaam had made peace with the world thus making war with God. Now, we are not studying angels in this book, but I believe this narrative gives us some insight into the real and present danger of how fallen angels (demons) and their leader, Satan, can be in our presence and we do not even realize it.

It is very rare that God will enable a person to visibly see demons. In scripture only Jesus Christ himself, saw the spirit form of Satan, during the temptation in the wilderness. But, God tells us enough about him that we can learn how our invisible enemy works and behaves.

Chapter 3

Who Is Satan?

We are going to begin our study by looking at Demons and their leader, called, Satan. This is where I choose to begin because this is where the Bible starts. We are introduced to Satan early in the Biblical account as a serpent in God's garden, Eden.

Before we pick up in the text let me warn you that there are basically two extremes that people fall into when it comes to the study of Satan and Demons. First is the tendency to underestimate Satan and his demons. I think this happens when we develop caricatures of Satan resembling a comic book villain.

These sorts of images are portrayed in Halloween costumes and school mascots. It makes you think that Satan is, at best, on par with leprechauns and unicorns and probably doesn't exist at all.

The other extreme is to overestimate Satan and his demons and bring them on par with God. You will find people who get fascinated, even obsessed, with this sort of thing.

In his book, "The Serpent of Paradise," Erwin Lutzer put it this way, "Just as a quarter lifted over the eye can obscure the blazing light of the sun, a star whose diameter is 865,575.9 miles, if we allow him, Satan will obscure our sight so that we forget God is infinitely bigger and more powerful."

William Gurnall offered a healthy perspective when he reminded us, "When God says, 'Stay,' Satan must stand like a dog by the table while the saints feast on God's comfort. He does not dare snatch even a tidbit, for the Master's eye is always upon him."

Remember, "the earth is the Lord's and the fullness thereof." (Psalms 24:1) *The sea is God's sea, the sky is God's sky, and the storm is God's storm. Martin Luther reminded us, "The Devil is God's devil." Erwin Lutzer said, "Blessed are those who understand that the prince of this world is the slave of the Prince of Peace."*

Satan in Pop Culture

You will probably be surprised how much of the stuff we think we know about Satan and his demons is found NOWHERE in the Bible. Most of our information came from secular fictional literature, movies, songs, etc. Here are a few examples:

Dante (1265-1321) in his classic work, "The Inferno," portrays Satan and his demons as tormenting the people who were cast into Hell. Scripture teaches that in all actuality, Satan will be enduring the wrath of God in Hell just as much as those who die without Christ.

The Devil will dish out no wrath, but, he will suffer the wrath of a holy God. He is not in Hell today, but rather does his work on the Earth along with multitudes of demons.

Milton (1608-1674) in his epic poem, "Paradise Lost and Paradise Regained," portrays Satan as a powerful and attractive personality that causes the reader to feel the seduction of darkness. Gradually, Milton reveals a more realistic perspective of Satan and exposes him as a deceiver.

Goethe (1749-1832) in his classic German legend, "Faust," gives a fictional account of Johann Georg Faust (1480-1540) who, in spite of being successful in life, is bored and sells his soul to the devil. Faust gives the devil a name, "Mephistopheles." In return for his soul, Satan would serve Faust on this earth, if Faust would be his servant in the world to come. The idea of a Satan who will help you succeed in life in return for your service has been a popular misunderstanding ever since.

Instead, the devil shares his "power" in safe, accepted ways. He predicts the future, gives us Ouija boards, Dungeons and Dragons, and performs a variety of parlor tricks for the unsuspecting masses.

Today, Satan and demons are depicted in practically every media format. According to the Rolling Stones, in "Sympathy for the Devil," he is a man of wealth and good taste. In the popular country music song, "The Devil Went Down to Georgia," by the Charlie Daniel's Band, Satan is a talented musician who enters fiddle playing contests in Georgia. Satan has been portrayed in over forty movies and many television shows. Satan has even made it onto the video game scene with a cameo appearance in "Guitar Hero III, Legends of Rock."

The devil has been at the center of a District Court Case. In 1971, Gerald Mayo brought a civil rights case against Satan in the Western District of Pennsylvania. Mr. Mayo alleged that, Satan plotted a scheme that caused his (Mr. Mayo's) downfall.

The suit stated, "Satan has on numerous occasions caused plaintiff misery and unwarranted threats, against the will of plaintiff. Satan has placed deliberate obstacles in his path and has caused plaintiff's downfall" and had therefore "deprived him of his constitutional rights." It was stated that such activity is prohibited under several acts of the U.S. Judicial Code.

Mr. Mayo asserted that he would not be able to afford the costs associated with his lawsuit and that they therefore should be waived. In the U. S. Court's written opinion, the court did not deny the existence of Satan. Instead, the court asserted that it was unlikely that Satan lived in Pennsylvania. They further stated that the devil was probably a resident of New Hampshire instead.

Therefore, he would thus fall under the jurisdiction of the latter state. There is no official paper record of this suit having ever transpired, but it is a source of lively folklore even still repeated today.

What Does the Bible Teach?

There are at least seventeen names and descriptors given to the Devil in scripture: Satan, Devil, Evil One, Great Red Dragon, Serpent of old, Abaddon, Apollyon, Adversary, Beelzebub, Belial, god of this world, ruler of this world, Prince of the power of the air, enemy, tempter, murderer, liar, and the accuser. Two Old Testament prophets talked in detail about the origin and fall of Satan.

Both of the prophets begin by prophesying about kings of their day. Then, they gradually begin to reveal a personality behind the king. The prophets address this personality, exposing that he can be nobody but Satan.

The first reveal is found in Ezekiel 28:11-19, where the Prophet seems to be referring to the King of Tyre; a coastal city to the North West of Israel.

Ezekiel 28:11-19 (NASB) *11 Again the word of the LORD came to me saying, 12 "Son of man, take up a lamentation over the king of Tyre and say to him, 'Thus says the Lord GOD,*

"You had the seal of perfection,

Full of wisdom and perfect in beauty.

13 "You were in Eden, the garden of God;

Every precious stone was your covering:

The ruby, the topaz and the diamond;

The beryl, the onyx and the jasper;

The lapis lazuli, the turquoise and the emerald;

And the gold, the workmanship of your settings and sockets,

Was in you.

On the day that you were created

They were prepared.

14 "You were the anointed cherub who covers,

And I placed you there.

You were on the holy mountain of God;

You walked in the midst of the stones of fire.

15 "You were blameless in your ways

From the day you were created

Until unrighteousness was found in you.

16 "By the abundance of your trade You were internally filled with violence,

And you sinned;

Therefore I have cast you as profane

From the mountain of God.

And I have destroyed you, O covering cherub,

From the midst of the stones of fire.

17 "Your heart was lifted up because of your beauty;

You corrupted your wisdom by reason of your splendor.

I cast you to the ground;

I put you before kings,

That they may see you.

18 "By the multitude of your iniquities,

In the unrighteousness of your trade

You profaned your sanctuaries.

Therefore I have brought fire from the midst of you;

It has consumed you,

And I have turned you to ashes on the earth

In the eyes of all who see you.

19 "All who know you among the peoples

Are appalled at you;

You have become terrified

And you will cease to be forever."""

Most Bible interpreters believe that Ezekiel 28:11–19 is two prophesies in one. Now, whatever the King of Tyre might have been, he was not perfect, he was not full of wisdom, nor was he likely to have been perfect in beauty.

Further, Tyre's King could not have been in Eden, so it seems to be obvious that Ezekiel was speaking to the personality who was empowering the King. Some scholars say that the king of Tyre was influenced, even possessed, by Satan, making the link between the two prophesies an even more relevant comparison.

Tyre was the epitome of wickedness and unscrupulous trade practices. By comparing the pride of the king of Tyre to the pride of Satan, a very forthright reference of evil is made. This being true, we see that Satan is not eternal like God. The Devil is not self- existent, but rather a created being. He is not omniscient, omnipresent or omnipotent.

When someone says, "Satan sure is giving me a fit today," probably not, he probably has bigger fish to fry than you or me. But, we do deal with his demons.

Ezekiel 28:14 *"You were the anointed cherub who covers, And I placed you there. You were on the holy mountain of God; You walked in the midst of the stones of fire."*

Some theologians agree that the verse in Ezekiel speaks of his (the devil before he was cast out) priestly duties.

He was the one who coordinated and led the heavens in congregational praise and worship of God the Father. His duty was to receive praise from creation and bring it before the creator as a gift to Him (God).

In Ezekiel 28:15 (NASV), we see the entry of sin into God's creation. *"You were blameless in your ways from the day you were created until unrighteousness was found in you."*

The word, "sin," is a term used in archery for, "missing the mark." Satan had sinned, "missed the mark," of God's righteousness. What, exactly, was Satan's sin?

Theologically, it is believed that the devil thought too highly of himself. You see, he had a great career and because of his exaggerated feelings of self-accomplishment, it would appear that he became bored.

Satan had the same problem that Alexander the Great had; he conquered the known world then sat and wept because there were no more worlds to conquer. In his own thinking, the devil had reached the pinnacle of leadership and the only higher position was that of God, Himself.

Not only did Satan have a great career, he also had great beauty. There is scriptural evidence that shows Lucifer was the most powerful and beautiful of all God's created beings.

Ezekiel 28:17 *"Your heart was lifted up because of your beauty; you corrupted your wisdom by reason of your splendor."*

Notice that the Devil's attractiveness trumped his common sense. That is so common in today's society. Young people who have a measure of beauty can find their physical good looks become a curse to them.

They have temptations and distractions in the world that take them away from their "first love," devotion to the Lord. This is a diversion that can be overcome with an active Godly influence and a family environment that is strong in Christ.

It appears Satan got to thinking as he was delivering the praise from creation to the Creator. "Why does God have to get all the praise? Sure, He should get most of it, but, shouldn't I get at least some of it; what does HE do, anyway?"

God is sovereign, He is Almighty, He doesn't need the approval or praise of anybody or anything. The Lord God Almighty does not have ego issues. A rose is not fragrant because it chooses to be, or needs to be; it is fragrant because it is—a rose.

Even so, God does not demand worship, God's presence causes worship. Scripture says (Luke 19:40) *if "we" don't praise Him, the rocks would cry out.* Not because God demands it—but because---they couldn't be silent.

Ezekiel put the physical consequences of Satan's rebellion against Almighty God into prophetic utterance.
(Ezekiel 28: 17b -19) *"Your heart was lifted up because of your beauty; you corrupted your wisdom by reason of your splendor.*
I cast you to the ground; I put you before kings,
That they may see you.
18 "By the multitude of your iniquities,
In the unrighteousness of your trade you profaned your sanctuaries. Therefore I have brought fire from the midst of you; it has consumed you,
And I have turned you to ashes on the earth
In the eyes of all who see you.
19 "All who know you among the peoples
are appalled at you; you have become terrified
And you will cease to be forever.""
****

The only thing that was greater in the heart of Satan than his career and beauty was his ambition. To gain some insight into the ambition of Satan, we must refer to another Prophet of old, Isaiah. In this passage, Isaiah is prophesying against the King of Babylon.

Like Ezekiel, Isaiah's prophesy seems to extend to more than just the King at hand and speak to the personality of Satan. The following statements are often referenced as the five "I WILL statements," assumed by the evil one.

Isaiah 14:13-14

"But you said in your heart,

I will ascend to heaven;

I will raise my throne above the stars of God,

I will sit on the mount of assembly in the recesses of the north.

I will ascend above the heights of the clouds;

I will make myself like the Most High."

****

Those self-aggrandizing statements are positive thinking at its best! Oprah would have been so proud. Satan could have sung the theme song for the "Laverne and Shirley" television sitcom (ABC 1976-1983) "Give us any chance, we'll take it. Give us any rule, we'll break it. We're gonna make our dreams come true. Doing it OUR way."

Satan wanted his best life now. He tapped in to the Power of Positive Thinking, joining the future ranks of Norman Vincent Peale and Robert Schuler. The Devil made the ultimate gamble, he gambled against God. But friend, a gamble against God is no gamble at all; it's suicide.

Regardless of the prize, it is foolish to gamble. The odds of hitting the jackpot in the Tennessee Lottery are one in seven million. (1 in 7,000,000). Those are ridiculous odds, but a few do win.

Friends, the odds of gambling against God are non-existent. Nobody wins against God; He is sovereign. Satan gambled against God and lost, setting into motion the law of unintended consequences. Gambling against God has been the epitome of Satanic thought since the very beginning of mankind.

Eve was tempted to gamble against God in the Garden. Satan tempted Jesus to gamble against the Father by placing temporal desires in front of His eternal calling. Then, Satan tempted Judas to gamble against God by handing Jesus over to the Pharisees.

Now, let's get personal, are you gambling against God? Basically, everyone is placing their bets for or against God with their life. Many are obviously putting their money on Satan and the world.

Others see no future in this world system and they are banking on Christ and the world to come.

Everyone is rebelling against something. You are either rebelling against God by doing things your way (Satan's way). Or you are rebelling against Satan and the world and doing things God's way.

Recently, I met a young lady who is dating a young man who is not a Christian and getting very serious with him. Their relationship is moving very speedily toward marriage.

God has clearly spoken that we are not to be unequally yoked together. This means we are not to marry a person who is an unbeliever. But, this girl was willing to gamble against God.

I also know a man who is still single well into adulthood because God has not yet brought a Godly Christian girl to him. He could have dozens of dates, but he is rebelling against Satan and waiting on God's best.

Don't gamble against God. The late Pastor, Dr. Adrian Rogers, said it well, "Sin will take your further than you want to go, cost you more than you want to pay and keep you longer than you wish to stay." That reality has been proven countless times in the lives of men and women who have married out of their faith.

What in the World is Satan Doing?

I recently read a story about a lady whose husband came home drunk and disorderly every night. He was making their lives miserable. She tried everything she knew to remedy the situation, but, nothing seemed to work. So, she said to herself, "I'll scare him out of his drinking habit."

One night while he was getting drunk, she put on a devil's costume. As usual, at two o'clock in the morning, he came through the front door drunk, as he had many times before. This time, however, she jumped in front of him with that devil costume on and said, "I'm the devil, you'd better be scared of me!"

"No," he said, "I'm not scared of you. I've been married to your sister for forty years."

The truth is, if you are a believer, there is no real need to fear the devil. Because *"greater is he that is in you than he that is in the world."* (I John 4:4) The Bible tells us not to fear, but to be sober and alert as we consider the enemy. The Apostle Peter said, in I Peter 5:8, *"Be of sober spirit, be on the alert. Your adversary, the devil, prowls around like a roaring lion, seeking someone to devour."*

Satan does not have your best interest at heart, but rather he desires to destroy those who bear the image of God; especially if you are redeemed by faith in His Messiah, Jesus Christ. So, it is wise to understand your enemy and his schemes against you.

In his autobiography, "Made in America," Sam Walton said that as he traveled from store to store to visit various Wal-Marts, he would often stop inside the local K-Mart stores. One might wonder why the CEO and founder of a large corporation would spend so much time in his competitor's store.

According to Walton, it was simply because he thought it wise to study his competition. In the same way, football coaches watch hours and hours of film of the opposing team prior to game day. Somewhere in Washington, D.C., people are studying the theology, philosophies and ideologies of Islam. They want to know all they can about the religion that the most extreme of our enemies adhere to.

You too, have an enemy; Satan has a strategy to destroy you and it is important for you to learn what it is. The Apostle Paul warned that we should not be ignorant of Satan's schemes (2 Corinthians 2:11).

To remedy our ignorance, we ought to learn about Satan and realize that he really doesn't have any new ideas. His old weapons still work the best; it is those old, successful weapons that the devil will typically use against you. The basic strategy of our enemy can be divided into two distinct parts.

I call these two parts, "The Ordinary," and "The Extraordinary" works of Satan and his demons. First, I will briefly describe both parts then throughout the remainder of the book, I will recount each part in greater detail.

The Extraordinary Works

The Church at Ephesus was accustomed to the extraordinary work of Satan. (Acts 19:11-16) *1 God continued to do extraordinary miracles through Paul. 12 When handkerchiefs and aprons that had touched his skin were taken to the sick, their diseases left them and evil spirits went out of them.*

13 Then some Jews who went around trying to drive out demons attempted to use the name of the Lord Jesus on those who had evil spirits, saying, "I command you by that Jesus whom Paul preaches!" 14 Seven sons of a Jewish high priest named Sceva were doing this.

15 But the evil spirit told them, "Jesus I know, and I am getting acquainted with Paul, but who are you?"

16 Then the man with the evil spirit jumped on them, got the better of them, and so violently overpowered all of them that they fled out of the house naked and bruised.

That report had to have been repeated often; when demons jump on people and beat them up, it would be difficult to keep it— quiet.

Extraordinary works are highlighted at Halloween, getting the most press with the most chatter. While there is much superstition and silliness, make no mistake, evil is not a thing of the past. It is perpetually personified in Satan and his demons. You would be wise not to make light of any work of the devil. Witchcraft is real, Satan worship is real. One of our children recently wanted to watch a show about "Wendy, the lovable Witch" and "Casper the Friendly Ghost." They couldn't understand why my wife and I wouldn't allow it.

I was able to bring the issue into perspective for our young ones when I asked them if they would want to watch a show about "Henry, the Loveable Devil Worshipper," and "Sally, the Nice Demonic Spirit." Would you want your children watching a cartoon about, "Joey, the Adorable Crack Head?"

No, that is ridiculous, unthinkable! Then, why do we allow our children to watch those who claim to practice witchcraft, in cartoons? As hard as Hollywood works to sanitize Satan's work, we must not forget that all the works of the devil are deadly and demonic.

<u>The Ordinary Works</u>

These are the areas where you battle Satan and demons day in and day out. These battles take place at work, at home, and sadly, even in the church. This is where Satan wants to cause division between husband and wife, between parents and children.

These "ordinary" places, where we go every day, are where Satan attempts to develop strongholds in our life. The evil intent is to make us feel absolutely helpless against temptation and think we are unable to turn away from a particular sin that presents itself. If the "sin" is presented to us every day, Satan thinks it is only a matter of time before we succumb to his wiles. He sets his traps in the midst of our everyday lives, and then waits for us to take the bait.

Satan has three objectives within the confines of the ordinary and extraordinary "works." The hoped for goals are, possession, obsession and temptation. The ultimate goal, after temptation, of course, is to completely control a person's thoughts, activities and will. Let's examine those three objectives and look at each individually.

Possession is where Satan or his demons take control of a creature's body and mind at will. This first happened in the Garden of Eden when Satan possessed one of God's creatures, the serpent, and used it for evil. God's Word shows us that humans are also potential candidates for possession.

A person who is possessed by the Devil may seem perfectly normal. Then, at the will of the demon, they will be controlled by evil; their voice and physical body given over to whatever Satan wants them to do and/or say.

After this momentary control, the demon is silent and the person usually doesn't even know what has happened.

A demonic possession is described in Mark 5:1-13

They came to the other side of the sea, into the country of the Gerasenes. 2 When He got out of the boat, immediately a man from the tombs with an unclean spirit met Him, 3 and he had his dwelling among the tombs. And no one was able to bind him anymore, even with a chain; 4 because he had often been bound with shackles and chains, and the chains had been torn apart by him and the shackles broken in pieces, and no one was strong enough to subdue him.

5 Constantly, night and day, he was screaming among the tombs and in the mountains, and gashing himself with stones.

6 Seeing Jesus from a distance, he ran up and bowed down before Him; 7 and shouting with a loud voice, he said, "What business do we have with each other, Jesus, Son of the Most High God? I implore You by God, do not torment me!"

8 For He had been saying to him, "Come out of the man, you unclean spirit!" 9 And He was asking him, "What is your name?" And he *said to Him, "My name is Legion; for we are many." 10 And he began to implore Him earnestly not to send them out of the country.

11 Now there was a large herd of swine feeding nearby on the mountain. 12 The demons implored Him, saying, "Send us into the swine so that we may enter them." 13 Jesus gave them permission. And coming out, the unclean spirits entered the swine; and the herd rushed down the steep bank into the sea, about two thousand of them; and they were drowned in the sea.

Let's look at the scripture a few lines at a time to understand what happened on that day.

(Mark 5:1-3) They came to the other side of the sea, into the country of the Gerasenes. 2 When He got out of the boat, immediately a man from the tombs with an unclean spirit met Him, 3 and he had his dwelling among the tombs.

Notice what marked this man and his state of demon possession. First, the man had retreated from the community (v 3a)

We can notice the man had an unnatural interest in death or he wouldn't be dwelling among the tombs. Some theologians even go as far as to speculate that the man had been feeding on the dead and decaying bodies, though that is not backed up by scripture.

A preoccupation, even a fascination, with death is often noticed in persons who are under the influence of demons. Later, we will talk about how death is a primary tool of Satan.

The demon possessed man also demonstrated spectacular abilities. In the last part of verse three and then verse four, we read, "--*And no one was able to bind him anymore, even with a chain; 4 because he had often been bound with shackles and chains, and the chains had been torn apart by him and the shackles broken in pieces, and no one was strong enough to subdue him.*" The demon had temporarily given this man superior strength.

In Acts 16:16 a demon had given a young girl the ability to tell fortunes. "It *happened that as we were going to the place of prayer, a slave-girl having a spirit of divination met us, who was bringing her masters much profit by fortune-telling.*"

It is not unusual for demons to give people temporary powers in and attempt to gain more and more control over them. When the demon finally claims full authority in a person's life, that life is decimated and they use their evil influence to take as many souls down with them as they possibly can.

The man wandering the tombs in the Gospel of Mark also suffered from physical and mental torment. Verse five says, "*Constantly, night and day, he was screaming among the tombs and in the mountains, and gashing himself with stones.*"

We must realize that demons despise humans because they bear the image of God and are loved by God. Satan and his demons want to hurt and abuse "us" in any way possible to show their hatred for God and to attempt to prove their domination over humanity, God's creation.

Once, while attending a conference in New Orleans, a friend and I journeyed into the French Quarter in order to present the Gospel to some who were celebrating Marti-Gras. We made our way to one alley where many people had set up tables to practice the magic arts. There were those who told fortunes, some who read palms and others who conducted séances. We talked to as many as would listen, but most would not.

One couple had a table where they were burning incense; they had an Ouija Board on display and seemed to be looking for conversation. After engaging in some small talk, I mentioned the fact that they obviously were "into spiritual things."

I asked, "Do you believe in life after death?" The lady replied, "Yes, we believe in Heaven."
"Wonderful!" I said, "What do you think it takes for a person to get to Heaven?"

The lady began to explain how "many roads lead to the same place." One person might find heaven through Catholicism and another through Wicca, but, "To each his own--."

It was at this point in the conversation that I simply said that scripture teaches differently. I asked her if it would be ok if I showed her a couple of passages that presented the exclusive nature of faith in the person and work of Jesus Christ.

As I opened my Bible, she began to grow increasingly uncomfortable. Her head was bobbing from side to side in a constant unbroken rhythm that can only be described as a seizure yet she never broke into the conversation.

We asked her if she was "ok," and she replied, "I'm fine." Ultimately, we shared the Gospel with her and prayed for her to find peace in the Lord Jesus Christ through His shed blood and the conquering of death, Hell and the grave.

Later, that same night, my friend and I were witnessing to a homeless man on a park bench. As we were sharing the Gospel,

we noticed that a stilt walker (a man walking on stilts) at least a hundred yards away had noticed us even though the park was very crowded.

My friend noticed the stilt walker was moving toward us yelling, "The Word, it burns!" Within a few moments, the walker had made his way to where we were ministering to the homeless man on the bench. Looking us in the eye, the man on stilts told us, "The Word, it burns, you need to leave!"

There are times when we see demons taking charge of a person's vocal capacities. Returning to our original passage in Mark 5, we read verses 6-7, "*6 Seeing Jesus from a distance, he ran up and bowed down before Him; 7 and shouting with a loud voice, he said, "What business do we have with each other, Jesus, Son of the Most High God? I implore You by God, do not torment me!"* This fevered request by the demon is not uncommon when confronted by the power of God.

Several times, in my ministry, I have noticed that in various congregations, during my sermon, especially when a strong effort has been made to reach the lost, and usually when I am speaking of the Lordship or sovereignty of Jesus Christ, an individual will become very uncomfortable; even at times, crying out.

A young lady in the church in South Alabama would scream every time I said, "The Lord, Jesus Christ." She seemed to be as surprised and uncomfortable by her outcry as anybody else in the room would be, but, it appeared to be beyond her control.

As we return to Mark 5 and continue to look at the demon possessed man wandering in the cemetery, we see that Jesus repeatedly commanded the demon to come out of the man. (v. 8-13)

8 For He had been saying to him, "Come out of the man, you unclean spirit!" 9 And He was asking him, "What is your name?" And he *said to Him, "My name is Legion; for we are many." 10 And he began to implore Him earnestly not to send them out of the country.

11 Now there was a large herd of swine feeding nearby on the mountain. 12 The demons implored Him, saying, "Send us into the swine so that we may enter them." 13 Jesus gave them permission. And coming out, the unclean spirits entered the swine; and the herd rushed down the steep bank into the sea, about two thousand of them; and they were drowned in the sea.

That is a classic case of demon possession. There is no record in scripture of a believer being possessed; there is no reason for a Christian to fear such things.

I believe when the Holy Spirit indwells a person, demonic spirits don't want to share the room. However, there is scripture that suggests every <u>un</u>believer is under Satan's mastery.

The Apostle Paul speaks of those, "*--in whose case the god of this world has blinded the minds of the unbelieving so that they might not see the light of the Gospel of the glory of Christ, who is the image of God.*" (2 Corinthians 4:4) *To this revelation, we must say, "Thanks be to God who can open blinded eyes."*

Alcoholism, Sexual Perversion, Gambling and other escapist sins are common weapons in the demons' toolbox arsenal of torment. While I said earlier that a Christian cannot be possessed, I do believe a Christian can be obsessed, demonized, influenced or oppressed.

The Apostle Paul, wrote in 2 Corinthians 12:7, *"Because of the surpassing greatness of the revelations, for this reason, to keep me from exalting myself, <u>there was given me a thorn in the flesh, a messenger of Satan to torment me</u> (underlining mine) to keep me from exalting myself."*

I cannot say conclusively what Paul was referring to or how this particular demon manifested itself. However, again, we are reminded that even in this affliction the demon was under the sharp oversight of a Sovereign God and was used to accomplish His purpose in the Apostle's life.

Today, the demonic toolbox is still used to torment God's children. The torments are the same; the tools have different names but are used to afflict the same distractions and sufferings. Let's examine those ancient yet still commonly used "tools."

<u>Obsession</u>, an idea or thought that continually preoccupies or intrudes on a person's mind, is a common demonic activity. I choose the word, obsession, rather than oppression or demonization (popular terms that refer to the same situation), because you are still very much in control despite what Satan wants you to believe.

Obsession is an unusual preoccupation or drive to commit a particular sin or to practice a particular attitude of disobedience. I Samuel tells of an instance of obsession with Saul, Israel's first King. I Samuel 16:14-15 *Now the Spirit of the Lord departed from Saul and an evil spirit from the Lord terrorized him. Saul's savants then said to him, "Behold now an evil spirit from God is terrorizing you."*

The demon would nudge Saul into fits of depression. It compelled Saul to attempt to kill David on several occasions as well as having the King to engage in talks with the witch of Endor. It is amazing that, under the influence of demons, the very thing Saul had outlawed, he himself was driven to engage in.

I don't think that is uncommon for demons to tempt a person in a particular area they are very much against. Perhaps this is why we hear of spiritual leaders who fall into the same sin they often rail against. Demon obsession is often revealed in different ways.

Cutting is when a disturbed, depressed or hurting person, (most commonly today, an adolescent, teen or young adult) uses a sharp object such as a knife, piece of glass, or other tool to literally cut themselves. The person believes the cut relieves tension that has built up internally to the point of having to do something to relieve the anxiety.

Though terribly misguided in their assumption, they think it is a "self –help" mechanism. You may be surprised to know that this bizarre behavior has been around for hundreds of years.
In the late 19th century, it is documented that women all over Europe were found to purposefully be puncturing themselves with sewing needles.

These incidents of women engaging in self-harm were seen as an odd medical phenomenon. Doctors recognized the bizarre behavior as a hysterical form of self-torture. Women who participated in this odd behavior were known as, "needle girls." (Alix Spiegel, NPR, "The History and Mentality of Self-Mutilation")

Until recently, cutting was believed to be a symptom of a borderline personality disorder. It was thought self-injury was a response to unstable moods, difficult circumstances, bad relationships and impulsive actions.

Cutting very rarely ever leads to suicide (fewer than 1%) leading Psychiatrists to believe the act of cutting is not a path to a permeant end, but rather a disorder of itself. Since the cutting is repeated over and over again, it can be assumed the person knows it will not kill them.

However, though self-harm is most commonly referenced today as "cutting," self-harm in general, also includes other forms. Abusive behavior such as self-beating, head banging, hair pulling, scratching and various forms of drug and alcohol abuse are sometimes found in the medical history of people who sometimes do eventually become suicidal. (Self-harm, Wikipedia)

I view such activity as a possible form of demon obsession. Whenever emotional pain is so intense the victim feels it necessary to do self-harm for relief; my first thought is that a demon's goal is to torment God's children. Emotional pain that is a path to physical pain instead of seeking God for help sounds like a tool from Satan's box of goodies.

Christianity Today tells the story of a young lady from Alabama who said, "When I think about how I cope with pain and loneliness, I think of a toolbox that only has two things inside; a razor blade and a bottle of rum."

Another commonly used tool from the demonic toolbox, both in ancient times and today, is, temptation. Temptation is when a demon uses your own natural inclination toward sin against you by providing an opportunity, then nudging you toward the disobedience.

Now, keep in mind that all temptation is not demonic; if there were no demons, we would still be tempted because we have a flesh nature. The capacity to sin was shown when Adam and Eve first gave in to the temptation in the Garden of Eden. God does not tempt anybody. (James 1:13) *"Let no man say when he is tempted, 'I am being tempted by God,' for God cannot be tempted with evil and he himself, tempts no one."*

God did not tempt Adam and Eve in the garden; the lust of their own flesh, the desire to know as much as God, led them into temptation. (Genesis 3:4-6) *4 But the serpent said to the woman, "You will not surely die. 5 For God knows that when you eat of it your eyes will be opened, and you will be like God, knowing good and evil."*

As I stated before, we don't need the influence of demons to be tempted. Our own desire for pleasure and knowledge can lead us into temptation. From the very beginning, God gave us the freedom to make choices.

Jesus, having been incarnated as fully God yet wholly man, was tempted. (Mark 1:13a) *"And he was in the wilderness forty days, being tempted by Satan."* ALL humankind face temptation and must choose to give in to the temptation, or turn aside. Jesus knows how temptation feels, and set the example for us.

The Apostle Paul, warns in I Corinthians 7:5, *"Do not deprive one another* (speaking of marital intimacy), *except perhaps by agreement for a limited time, that you may devote yourselves to prayer; but then come together again,* (Why?) *so that Satan may not tempt you because of your lack of self-control."* (parentheses inserts mine)

Earlier, I stated that a Christian cannot be "possessed," but they can be obsessed and obviously, Christians are often tempted. We must learn to discern whether temptation is demonic, or coming from our own flesh so we can take appropriate actions to handle each temptation.

As you look closely at the scripture, you can begin to discern the difference between a human flesh temptation and a demonic temptation. When Satan tempted Jesus during the 40 days in the wilderness, the temptation had both a physical (flesh) temptation and a demonic temptation.

The flesh temptation first came through physical need, a flesh weakness.

(Matthew 4:1-4) *Then Jesus was led up by the Spirit into the wilderness to be tempted by the devil. 2 And after fasting forty days and forty nights, he was hungry. 3 And the tempter came and said to him, "If you are the Son of God, command these stones to become loaves of bread." 4 But he answered, "It is written," 'Man shall not live by bread alone, but by every word that comes from the mouth of God.'"*

Jesus knew God's plan of the cross and the payment for sin, and so did the devil. The last temptation presented to Jesus was, (Matthew 4:8-10) *"8 Again, the devil took him to a very high mountain and showed him all the kingdoms of the world and their glory. 9 And he said to him, "All these I will give you, if you will fall down and worship me." 10 Then Jesus said to him, "Be gone, Satan! For it is written, "'You shall worship the Lord your God and him only shall you serve.'"*

Again, the temptation given had both a physical and a spiritual/demonic temptation. The flesh lusts for power and authority. Read the scriptures again. Can you see what the spiritual/demonic temptation was? As humans, we are well aware of the physical temptations of hunger and power. The demonic temptation is more subtle; to question the sovereignty of God. "Did God really say that? Are you sure? Why would God allow this?"

Jesus' response with each of Satan's attempts was the very same and covered both the flesh and the demonic temptation. On every temptation, Jesus' response was, "AS IT IS WRITTEN—." He pointed back to the sovereignty of God.

Now, think, where is our, your, greatest weakness? That would be the flesh part where demons attack you. Pay attention, now that you know this is a set up; you will see that Satan will over play his hand.

Pastor and author, Chuck Swindol, told of getting in an elevator after a long day of ministry away from his wife and family. An attractive young woman stepped into the elevator with him and offered him a "date," for a price. Thankfully, the Pastor, aware of the flesh weakness and the spiritual temptation, was able to turn aside and not fall into the trap.

When I was a single college student traveling home from a night of worship with our Baptist campus ministry, I remember passing a stack of adult magazines lying on the sidewalk. Each page was flipping in the wind so that the contents were obvious. Can you see the set up? Thankfully, so did I and the "trap" was useless.

In a later chapter, we will study what the destiny of Satan is.

The Apostle Paul, said that *"---no advantage would be taken of us by Satan, for we are not ignorant of his schemes."* (2 Corinthians 2:11)

Chapter 4

How to Deal With Demons

1. Recognize God's Hand. Remember, I said earlier that Satan is not entirely a free agent. He is under the careful oversight of a God that loves you deeply. God will allow Satan to go no further than that which can ultimately be used in conforming you into the image of Christ.

In the life of Job, God used Satan to refine and prove his (Job's) faith. The Apostle Paul, writing to the Church at Corinth, said in I Corinthians 5:5 *"I have decided to deliver such a one to Satan for the destruction of his flesh, so that his spirit may be saved in the day of the Lord Jesus."* (NASB)

Paul received a thorn in the flesh, a messenger from Satan to buffet him lest he become puffed up. Ask yourself, "What might God be trying to do through this?"

Sometimes, it takes a fresh set of eyes to discover if and what the lesson is. You may need to seek a Biblical counselor to help you gain perspective on what God is developing in your life or teaching through your circumstances.

2. Recognize the extent in your potential of freedom. It is important that you realize that you cannot ultimately banish demons from your presence. Even our Lord had to battle Satan and demons.

That is what frustrates me with all these people who are constantly binding Satan; he keeps getting loose! This is what you are promised in I Corinthians 10:13, *"No temptation has overtaken you but such as is common to man; and God is faithful, who will not allow you to be tempted beyond what you are able, but with the temptation will provide the way of escape also, so that you will be able to endure it."* (NASB)

God will govern the temptation so that you can bear it AND provide a way of escape for you.

An on-line thesaurus defines "narrow escape" as, "a situation in which an accident or other unfortunate incident is barely avoided." The narrow escape in Biblical times would refer to a narrow corridor on a sharp cliff that one might find in the Judean countryside.

This knowledge might be useful as a mental trigger to remind you of something you could turn your focus to. This change of focus could come as a phone call received just in the nick of time before you made a sinful decision. However, the "escape" manifests itself; recognize it as being from the hand of God.

3. Resist the Devil. *"Submit therefore to God. Resist the devil and he will flee from you."* (James 4:7) NASB

Resisting is to be understood in its fullest sense; as an action of striving against an adversary. Put on the full armor of God, a practice that will be discussed in detail in a later chapter.

<u>Concluding thoughts</u>. A fish out of water might get to the place where that is seems almost dead. However, once you put it in the water it propels into the depths with passion to survive.

You are the same way. You were created to have a passionate relationship with Jesus; some of you don't even know that. But, today, that could all change. You could get into the water you were born for IN CHRIST, where you have all you need to wreak havoc on the devil.

Chapter 5

The Battle

Nothing compares with the experience of watching a football game at the University of Alabama. I had an opportunity to watch the 2009 team (they went on to become National Champions) defeat the University of Tennessee. Now, I have to say, that was the first game I had attended in 25 years.

Picture this scenerio, 90,000 passionate fans and a guy dressed up like TIDE washing detergent. The guys I went with were literally shaking with nervous excitement. We watched the walk of champions where these massive guys entered the stadium. 6'5", 365 pounds and MOUNT Terrance Cody!

This guy can hurt somebody permanently. Now, imagine that you were lining up against Terrance Cody, you a 14 year old girl, a 50 year old man, whatever it's you. Imagine you had no pads, he's going to hit you full force.

What if Terrance Cody had a sword and order to take off your head? You wouldn't dare line up against Mt. Cody without some protection! Never the less, every day many of us try to face a far greater foe as we go to war against Satan and demons without our armor.

Everyone is living in one of two battles. To make peace with the Devil is to make war with Christ. To make peace with Christ is to make war with the Devil. The Christian life is a war.

o   When the Apostle Paul, came to the end of his life, he said in 2 Timothy 4:7, *"I have fought the good fight, I have finished the race, I have kept the faith."*

o   In I Timothy 6:12, Paul tells Timothy, *"Fight the good fight of faith; lay hold on eternal life to which you were called."*

o   Concerning his own life of warfare, Paul said *"I do not run aimlessly, I do not box as one beating the air; but I pommel my body and subdue it, lest after preaching to others I myself should be disqualified."* (I Corinthians 9:26-27)

o   Concerning his ministry Paul said, *"Though we live in the world we are not carrying on a worldly war, for the weapons of our warfare are not worldly but have divine power to destroy strongholds. We destroy arguments and ever proud obstacle to the knowledge of God and take every thought captive to obey Christ."* (2 Corinthians 10:3-5)

Make no mistake about it, to make peace with Christ is to make war with Satan. There is a war going on today greater than any conflict of WWII. You have an enemy that is more crafty, devious and threatening than Communism or militant Islam.

In this conflict the casualties do not merely lose an arm or an eye or an earthly life. They lose everything; this battle is for the souls of all humanity. Until you understand and believe this, you will not pray or give as you ought, or serve as you ought.

You will be a self-centered consumerist American Christian that goes to your grave whining like a baby for a bottle. Meantime, spiritual battles are being won and lost all around you.

Nowhere in the Bible does God call us to prepare for the impending warfare any more than in Ephesians 6. The context of the passage gives you some indication of where the warfare takes place.

The scripture just finished teaching about the home, rules for the family and the workplace. It's in the everydayness of life you will encounter tremendous conflict. You say, "Well Pastor, I thought the battle was won on the cross?" In a very real sense it was; but Satan has not yet conceded defeat.

It is as if you and I live between D-Day (June 6, 1944) and V.E. Day (May 8, 1945). During that time, between the two Historic events, is when the battle of the bulge was fought. Students of World War 2 have often remarked that although VE-Day was not until May 8, 1945, in a very real sense the war in Europe was over on June 6, 1944 — D-Day.

*"In "Operation Overlord" some 1,000 ships — the largest armada ever to set sail — carried roughly 200,000 soldiers across the English Chanel to France where they stormed the coasts of Normandy. This was only the beginning of a military buildup that Germany could never have stopped.

Anyone watching objectively knew that it was not only a matter of time — not if, but when. The amassing of such military personnel and material, the relentless crushing of German factories from American aircraft, the ever narrowing of Germany's supply lines — all this declared that the difference between D-Day and VE-Day was just a matter of time."

*(Credo Magazine, Fred Zaspel, September 12, 2013, Professor of Systematic Theology at Calvary Baptist Seminary in Lansdale, PA. the author of The Theology of B.B. Warfield: A Systematic Summary and Warfield on the Christian Life: Living in Light of the Gospel.)

The Enemy gets the most fierce when he is cornered. He starts breaking out the roadside bombs, engages in guerilla warfare. He uses human shields and the rules of war go out the window. John said it well in Revelation 12:12 *For this reason, rejoice, O heavens and you who dwell in them. Woe to the earth and the sea, because the devil has come down to you, having great wrath, knowing that he has only a short time."* (NASB)

So, what are we to do? The Apostle Paul wrote in Ephesians 6:10-13 *"10 Finally, be strong in the Lord and in the strength of His might. 11 Put on the full armor of God, so that you will be able to stand firm against the schemes of the devil. 12 For our struggle is not against flesh and blood, but against the rulers, against the powers, against the world forces of this darkness, against the spiritual forces of wickedness in the heavenly places. 13 Therefore, take up the full armor of God, so that you will be able to resist in the evil day, and having done everything, to stand firm."*

Throughout the book of Ephesians, it seems that the Apostle begs you not to stand in your own strength, and not to use your own weapons. Why? Your own knowledge and strength is not sufficient for this battle. That statement flies right in the face of everything that we are taught through secular humanism.

In February 2010, self-help guru, James Author Ray was arrested for leading 50+ of his followers into a Native American Sweat Lodge on a New Age Retreat. His goal was to teach them their personal capacity to overcome adversity and achieve true greatness and success.

Nobody thought to check the oxygen levels in the "sweat lodge," resulting in the death of three people and the hospitalization of nineteen. In 2011 he was sentenced to prison for negligent homicide in the death of the three people.

He served two years in an Arizona State Prison and was released under supervision. Mr. Ray was not an evil man; his intent was to help people. Planning in his own strength and knowledge cost him a great price.

Scripture sums the unfortunate event up perfectly. Proverbs 19:2 *"It is dangerous to have zeal without knowledge, and the one who acts hastily makes poor choices."* The details of Mr. Ray's well-intentioned but disastrous event can be read here: https://en.wikipedia.org/wiki/James_Arthur_Ray

James Ray was one of many self-help gurus featured on the movie, "The Secret," produced after the skyrocketing success of the book by the same title. The tenet of the book is that an individual's focused positive thinking can result in life changing results.

These results are supposedly manifested in increased wealth, health, happiness and more. Oprah Winfrey said, "The universe, God, whatever you choose to call it, only supports you in your (own) greatness." (parenthesis mine)

Her statement sounds benign, even possible, however, that ideology flies in the face of, and directly contradicts, everything the Word of God teaches. My friends, according to God's Word, you are the biggest problem you have, you are not the answer to your problems! You ARE the problem.

The scripture reveals that the answer is not found in improving self, but by crucifying self and allow Christ to live in you and through you. That is exactly what the Apostle Paul, said in our earlier text, *"finally, be strong in the Lord and in the strength of His might. Put on the full armor of God."*

We don't stand in our own strength, dressed in our own armor; we stand in HIS strength wearing HIS armor. When you read Paul's prayers throughout Ephesians, he repeatedly reminds us that we are to rest in the power of God, not in our own strength. John the Baptist, had it right, *"I must decrease, He must increase."* (John 3:30)

Why did Paul constantly pray that we would rely on God's power and strength? Ephesians 6:11b says, *"--- so that you will be able to stand firm against the schemes of the devil."*

Remember in Genesis 3:1a said, *"Now the serpent was more crafty than any beast of the field which the LORD God had made."* The Devil has schemes and crafty methods that are designed to render you helpless and ineffective in your work for the Lord.

He does not mind that you have a nice home, he doesn't mind if you drive a new car. He just wants you to keep your mouth shut about Jesus. If you refuse to be silent about Christ's blessings and provisions, Satan will do everything he can to make you and your testimony look foolish. And, by the way, in your own strength, you don't have a chance of preventing his efforts. The struggle is not of this world, it is spiritual.

Ephesians 6:12 *"For our struggle is not against flesh and blood, but against the rulers, against the powers, against the world forces of this darkness, against the spiritual forces of wickedness in the heavenly places."*

In other words, there are demons aligned in every area against us; the battle can't be fought in our own strength. Satan and his demons have several tools in their arsenal. Listed here are a few I'm sure we are all familiar with.

<u>Persecution</u>
When you are doing everything you know of to serve Christ, demons will provoke others to attack you.

Matthew 10:16-23 16 *"Behold, I send you out as sheep in the midst of wolves; so be shrewd as serpents and innocent as doves. 17 But beware of men, for they will hand you over to the courts and scourge you in their synagogues; 18 and you will even be brought before governors and kings for My sake, as a testimony to them and to the Gentiles. 19 But when they hand you over, do not worry about how or what you are to say; for it will be given you in that hour what you are to say. 20 For it is not you who speak, but it is the Spirit of your Father who speaks in you.*

21 "Brother will betray brother to death, and a father his child; and children will rise up against parents and cause them to be put to death. 22 You will be hated by all because of My name, but it is the one who has endured to the end who will be saved.

23 "But whenever they persecute you in one city, flee to the next; for truly I say to you, you will not finish going through the cities of Israel until the Son of Man comes."

Distraction

The Devil loves to get you off focus, so he will stir something up to distract you. I think we've all sat down for our "quiet time" with our Lord only to find you are thinking about everything else, except prayer. When we finally get focused on undistracted conversation, we remember to talk to God about everything from activities to zeal. Then, we realize we haven't asked for opportunity to tell others about Jesus. Satan wants us to be so—busy—that we neglect our primary calling; to win souls for Christ.

Accusation

The Devil will sometimes level unfounded accusations against you. He did it to Job, then Paul, Peter and even to Jesus. Scripture says that Satan is the accuser of the brethren.

Revelation 12:10 *"Then I heard a loud voice in heaven, saying, 'Now the salvation, and the power, and the kingdom of our God and the authority of His Christ have come, for the accuser of our brethren has been thrown down, he who accuses them before our God day and night.'"*

A friend of mine, a Pastor, made mention of a woman in his community who accused him of being "stuck up," because she spoke to him while he was out in his yard mowing the lawn and he didn't respond to her greeting.

The woman was well known for her walks through the neighborhood while scantily attired. Perhaps she was disappointed that the Pastor made no notice of her attention seeking wardrobe. Or maybe she honestly had no idea that her appearance was distracting to most people in the neighborhood.

Whatever her personal issues, she told neighbors that the Pastor failed to speak to her and her feelings were hurt. Of course, word got back to the Pastor. The Pastor, having heard the story of the disgruntled woman, made sure he threw up his hand and waved at her the next time she passed him on the street.

In response to his efforts, the dear woman told everybody in town that the Pastor had flirted with her while she was out walking. Sometimes you can't win, no matter what you do; give it to Jesus.

Temptation

Sometimes, the Devil will just out right tempt a Christian to do evil. James 1:13 says, *"Let no one say when he is tempted, "I am being tempted by God"; for God cannot be tempted by evil, and He Himself does not tempt anyone."* So, rest assured that ANY temptation that comes before you is not brought by God as a test.

Satan knows you are a child of God. He also knows your weaknesses. What do you think of when you think of, "sin?" Stealing, murder, adultery, homosexuality (?) obviously the Devil will have no luck—hopefully—no luck—tempting Christians with the obvious sins.

As Christians, we seem to focus on only specific sins, those that are obviously---well---sinful. However, scripture has a much more inclusive list, a list that may make even the most committed of us chew our bottom lip and squirm in our seat.

Galatians 5:19-21 *The (sinful) acts of the flesh are obvious: sexual immorality, impurity and debauchery; idolatry and witchcraft; hatred, discord, jealousy, fits of rage, selfish ambition, dissensions, factions and envy; drunkenness, orgies, and the like.*
I warn you, as I did before, that those who live like this will not inherit the kingdom of God. (underlining mine)

Scripture reveals an even more eye opening look at the nature of sin. It is easy to blame our temptations on the Devil. However, and I do believe I mentioned this earlier in this book, sometimes, maybe even—often, (?) Satan has nothing to do with our temptation. James 1:14 *But each one is tempted when he is carried away and enticed by his own lust.* (ouch) As the Psalmist David would say, (selah) or, "think on this."

Discouragement

Discouragement is also a powerful weapon of Satan. Having a group of believers surround us as encouragers is extremely important. There are some who say they don't need to physically attend church; they can watch preaching on television.
I'm so thankful for televangelists who feed those who are unable to physically get up, get out and show up in the sanctuary. Our own services and many, if not most, churches are now available on live feed. This makes worship in our easy chair while still in our pajamas with a cup of coffee and a piece of jelly toast even more—tempting. Never the less, we need—fellowship.

Hebrews 10:23-25 addresses that very issue. "*23 Let us hold fast the confession of our hope without wavering, for He who promised is faithful; 24 and let us consider how to stimulate one another to love and good deeds, 25 not forsaking our own assembling together, as is the habit of some, but encouraging one another; and all the more as you see the day drawing near.*"

Satan knows if he can separate you from the fellowship of believers, he can whisper that you are alone. Nobody understands your circumstances; your hope is futile. This can open the door for depression.

Once we are isolated from our encouragers, bitterness and anger can set in. ANY thought that tells you that you are alone, hopeless and left out is the voice of Satan. The Word of God has answers for discouragement; fellowship is one of them.

Failure of Others

As Christians, we are to look to Christ for leadership. One place to find strong Christ leadership is to look to proven leaders that we are to emulate, Hebrews 13:7 7 *Remember those who led you, who spoke the word of God to you; and considering the result of their conduct, imitate their faith.*

We must be cautious to discern the Christ like attributes of our leaders and be aware that those in positions of leadership are in the bullseye range of Satan's target. Why? If the Devil can bring down a Christ leader, the ripple effect can ruin the faith of many.

Imagine the damage if one of the church staff or a prominent leader in the congregation fell to the wiles of Satan. The damaged lives would be many; damage control would be a monumental task.

According to scripture, God holds persons in positions of leadership to a higher standard. *"Let not many of you become teachers, (leaders) my brethren, knowing that as such we will incur a stricter judgment."* (James 3:1) (parentheses mine)

A quick reminder that God is faithful to uphold us in our temptations, but it is, we, in the end, that makes the decision to embrace temptation or ---flee from it. The higher standard of leadership and our caution in blindly following leaders without discernment aside, you are also a leader.

Perhaps you are not in a formal position of leadership, but, even so, the Apostle Paul had instructions for you as well. *"Follow my example, as I follow the example of Christ."* (I Corinthians 11:1) (NIV)

Chapter 6

What is the Solution?

(I Peter 5:8) *"Be of sober spirit, be on the alert. Your adversary, the devil, prowls around like a roaring lion, seeking someone to devour."*

(Ephesians 6:10-17) *"10 Finally, be strong in the Lord and in the strength of His might. 11 Put on the full armor of God, so that you will be able to stand firm against the schemes of the devil. 12 For our struggle is not against flesh and blood, but against the rulers, against the powers, against the world forces of this darkness, against the spiritual forces of wickedness in the heavenly places.*

13 Therefore, take up the full armor of God, so that you will be able to resist in the evil day, and having done everything, to stand firm. 14 Stand firm therefore, having gird your loins with truth, and having put on the breastplate of righteousness, 15 and having shod your feet with the preparation of the gospel of peace; 16in addition to all, taking up the shield of faith with which you will be able to extinguish all the flaming arrows of the evil one. 17 And take the helmet of salvation, and the sword of the Spirit, which is the word of God."

How often have we heard the "armor of God" scripture quoted? When I hear that sermon lesson, I always imagined the Apostle Paul glancing at the Roman Guard who had him in chains and making an analogy to spiritual warfare. That is very unlikely for a couple of reasons.

1. It is unlikely that a Roman soldier would be dressed in full battle gear while simply guarding a prisoner in a secure cell.

2. I believe Paul was probably thinking about the depiction of the Messiah in the book of Isaiah. The spiritual "armor" analogy fits the scriptures very well.

- (Isaiah 11:4-5) *"But with righteousness He will judge the poor, and decide with fairness for the afflicted of the earth; and He will strike the earth with the rod of His mouth, and with the breath of His lips He will slay the wicked. 5 Also righteousness will be the belt about His loins, and faithfulness the belt about His waist."*

- (Isaiah 59:17) *"He put on righteousness like a breastplate, and a helmet of salvation on His head; and He put on garments of vengeance for clothing and wrapped Himself with zeal as a mantle."*

- (Isaiah 49:2) *"He has made My mouth like a sharp sword, In the shadow of His hand He has concealed Me; and He has also made Me a select arrow, He has hidden Me in His quiver."*

- (Isaiah 52:7) *"How lovely on the mountains are the feet of him who brings good news, who announces peace and brings good news of happiness, who announces salvation, and says to Zion, 'Your God reigns!'"*

Clearly, the spiritual "full armor of God" is Paul's analogy of Yahweh's own armor! God has provided the armor that He and His Messiah wore for God's people, you and me, as we engage in battle. Paul instructed us to wear the armor of God every day; he said, "put it on," not sometimes, not for specific circumstances, just "put it on."

Ask yourself this question, right now, are you trying to fight the Devil in your own sufficiency, or are you dying to "self" and donning the full armor of God? Sadly, there are Christians who do not even know we have armor we can wear when we face Satan.

Let's take a look at this armor and how it protects us.

Chapter 7

The Armor of God

Now that you know we actually are involved in Spiritual Warfare, let us explore what that means in our everyday Christ life. I read about a man who had too much to drink and was driving the wrong way on a one way street. A police officer pulled him over and said, "Hey, buddy, didn't you see the arrows?"

The drunken man slurred, "Man, I didn't even see the Indians!" We may not be aware of a war, however, the conflict is real; many of us are getting wounded and possibly losing this battle.

I know what you are thinking, "But—I thought the battle was won at Calvary!" Dan and Brenda J. Robinson with Labron and Brooke Cason, in their book, "Time in the Garden: Making His Heart Mine," explain it perfectly. "Satan has already been defeated through the work of Jesus Christ, at Calvary! The war has been won, but the battle still rages. We must, therefore, "---*endure hardness as a good soldier of Jesus Christ,* (2Timothy 2:3)" having faith in the blessed fact that God is our Protector and Deliverer and He will fight the battle for us."

Jeffery C. Ward in his book, "The Civil War," recounts a scene that took place on a battlefield during the battle of Gettysburg. All of the staff was standing around talking about Robert E. Lee. They were remarking that General Lee could, "do this," and "do that."

Ulysses S. Grant heard all he wanted to hear and finally said to them, "I am tired of hearing about Robert E. Lee. You would think he was going to do a double somersault and land in our rear. I want you to quit thinking about what he is going to do to you and I want you to start thinking about what you're going to do to him."

The Bible makes it explicitly clear that compared to you, the enemy is a formidable foe. BUT, compared to Christ, he is only a bothersome flea. Whatever your battle is, it is a battle that you CAN win.

Your marriage does not have to fail, your children don't have to rebel and your job doesn't have to be a depressing prison. You do not have to be a slave to sin. As a matter of fact, you can personally go on the offence and take new ground for the Kingdom of Christ!

Not only can you change your own circumstances, you can lead others to freedom. It's time we begin thinking about what we can do to the devil instead of what he can do to us. However, in order to win, you must first understand the benefits of the armor that God has provided for you.

Nowhere in the Bible is your spiritual armor described better than Ephesians, chapter 6. In this chapter, Paul has moved away from his theological discourse of chapters 1-3 and is moving away from the practical discussion of chapters 4-5.

Paul wrote the first half of the letter to the Ephesians like a seminary professor, the second half he wrote like a Biblical counselor. He wrote the final portion as if a great African American preacher had called all of his literary tools and passion into use.

Take note that Paul wrote it with a fervor that was meant to arouse and motivate the congregation to action.

(Ephesians 6:10-18) *"10 Finally, be strong in the Lord and in the strength of His might. 11 Put on the full armor of God, so that you will be able to stand firm against the schemes of the devil. 12 For our struggle is not against flesh and blood, but against the rulers, against the powers, against the world forces of this darkness, against the spiritual forces of wickedness in the heavenly places.*

13 Therefore, take up the full armor of God, so that you will be able to resist in the evil day, and having done everything, to stand firm. 14 Stand firm therefore, HAVING GIRDED YOUR LOINS

WITH TRUTH, and HAVING PUT ON THE BREASTPLATE OF RIGHTEOUSNESS, 15 and having shod YOUR FEET WITH THE PREPARATION OF THE GOSPEL OF PEACE; 16in addition to all, taking up the shield of faith with which you will be able to extinguish all the flaming arrows of the evil one.

17 And take THE HELMET OF SALVATION, and the sword of the Spirit, which is the word of God. 18 With all prayer and petition pray at all times in the Spirit, and with this in view, be on the alert with all perseverance and petition for all the saints—" (emphasis mine)

As I stated earlier, verse 11 (put on the full armor-) is meant as, "keep it on." There are no furloughs; there are no truces, no leaves of absence, no command to cease fire. You are to keep your armor on and your guard up. If you let your guard down, Satan will surely sucker punch you. He will hit you at your weakest moment when you least expect it.

Why are we to keep the full armor of God on at all times? Verse 11b-13 says, *"so that you will be able to stand firm against the schemes of the devil. 12 For our struggle is not against flesh and blood, but against the rulers, against the powers, against the world forces of this darkness, against the spiritual forces of wickedness in the heavenly places. 13 Therefore, take up the full armor of God, so that you will be able to resist in the evil day, and having done everything, to stand firm."*

God has given us the armor guaranteed to repulse the most powerful missiles, strongest bombs and the mightiest torpedoes the Devil can throw at you in the Spirit world. The Apostle James spoke well, (James 4:7) *"Resist the devil and he will free from you."*

Had you noticed there is not even one verse in the Bible that tells us to run from the devil? The Bible says we are to flee temptation and sin, but never are we instructed to flee from our enemy, Satan.
Instead, scripture instructs us to resist the Devil and <u>he will flee from us</u>. Now, let's take a look at each piece of armor that God has given us to wear for our protection.

1. The Belt of Truth

Ephesians 6:14a says, *"Stand firm therefore, HAVING GIRDED YOUR LOINS WITH TRUTH--."* (emphasis mine) The Prophet Isaiah tells us in chapter 11:5 that Yahweh's Messiah wears a belt. *"Also righteousness will be the belt about His loins, and faithfulness the belt about His waist."*

Our God is not flippant, ruthless or maniacal as many of the pagan deities are said to have been. NO, he wears the belt of righteousness and faithfulness; as Paul put it, the belt of truth. The Greek word Paul uses for "truth" is "Alethia." It refers to inward truth, truth of heart or sincerity as opposed to objective truth which we will find later used to describe the sword of the Spirit.

The Roman Soldier's belt and tunic: "The Roman soldier always wore a tunic, an outer garment that serves as his primary clothing. It was usually made of a large, square piece of material with holes cut out for the head and arms. Ordinarily it draped loosely over most of the soldier's body.

Since the greatest part of ancient combat was hand-to-hand, a loose tunic was a potential hindrance and even a danger. Before a battle it was therefore carefully cinched up and tucked into the heavy leather belt that girded the soldier's loins." (The MacArthur New Testament Commentary, Moody Publishers, "The Girdle of Truth.")

o In Hebrews, we are instructed to gird up. (Hebrews 12:1b) *"-let us also lay aside every encumbrance and the sin which so easily entangles us, and let us run with endurance the race that is set before us"*

o This "girding up" or preparing oneself for battle is what the Apostle Paul refers in (2 Timothy 2:4) *"No soldier in active service entangles himself in the affairs of everyday life, so that he may please the one who enlisted him as a soldier."*

What does it mean to "gird your loins with truth?" I believe that Paul is calling the soldier of Christ to a pure and sincere devotion of conscience to the Lord Jesus Christ.

I Corinthians 12:20 lists some issues that should not be pleasing if found in a Christ centered life. *"20 For I am afraid that perhaps when I come I may find you to be not what I wish and may be found by you to be not what you wish; that perhaps there will be strife, jealousy, angry tempers, disputes, slanders, gossip, arrogance, disturbances—"*

In modern day terms, these hindrances to speak freely and openly about your love and faith for the Lord Jesus could be; you've gossiped about somebody, or caused strife by continuously turning everything into an argument. Maybe you are giving in to the temptation to tell naughty jokes or look on a woman, other than your wife, with lust?

Paul is saying do not get tangled up in that "stuff." Gird your loins with the belt of a good conscience and integrity. Some of us here, today, need to appeal to God for help in keeping a clean conscience in a dirty world.

2. The Breastplate of Righteousness

(Ephesians 6:14) *Stand firm therefore, HAVING GIRDED YOUR LOINS WITH TRUTH and HAVING PUT ON THE BREASTPLATE OF RIGHTEOUSNESS"* (emphasis mine)

Paul's analogy comes from Isaiah 59:17, *"He put on righteousness like a breastplate—"*

No Roman soldier would go into battle without his breastplate, a tough sleeveless piece of armor that covered his full torso. It was often made of leather or heavy linen, onto which were sewn overlapping slices of animal hooves or horns or pieces of metal.

Some were made of large pieces of metal, molded or hammered to conform to the body. The purpose of that piece of armor is obvious, to protect the heart, lungs, intestines, and other vital organs." (The MacArthur New Testament Commentary, Moody Publishers, The Breastplate of Righteousness)

The ancient Jews believed that the heart represented the mind and will, while the bowels were thought to be the seat of emotions and feelings. It is at the vulnerable areas that Satan launches his deadliest weapons. He wants to affect your mind, your will, and your emotions, areas that would (should!) be protected by the breastplate of righteousness.

The Bible refers to three types of righteousness.
<u>Self-righteousness</u>. There is no scripture directly saying this is the worst type of sin, however, there are scriptures that suggest the act of "having" self-righteousness is not a desirable attribute. Two that come to mind that suggest this are:

(Luke 18:9) *And He also told this parable to some people who trusted in themselves that they were righteous, and viewed others with contempt:*

(Revelation 3:17-18) *Because you say, "I am rich, and have become wealthy, and have need of nothing," and you do not know that you are wretched and miserable and poor and blind and naked, I advise you to buy from Me gold refined by fire so that you may become rich, and white garments so that you may clothe yourself, and that the shame of your nakedness will not be revealed; and eye salve to anoint your eyes so that you may see."*

Sadly, the belief in self-righteousness doesn't seem to be easily recognized in oneself. Yet, it is the very thing that some (many?) people have. Arrogance and pride are good indicators of thinking their own accomplishments will gain God's approval and reward.

Imputed Righteousness is God's perfect righteousness imputed at conversion. Imputed means to ascribe righteousness to somebody by virtue of a similar quality in another; in theology having a relationship with Christ imputes righteousness to a believer. (on-line dictionary)

(2 Corinthians 5:21) *" He made Him who knew no sin to be sin on our behalf, so that we might become the righteousness of God in Him."* This freely given righteousness delivers us from eternity in Hell, but it does not prevent Satan from messing with us.

<u>Practical Righteousness</u>. The breastplate of righteousness we put on every day as part of our spiritual armor used against our adversary is our practical righteousness. This type of righteousness is seen in a life lived in obedience to God's Word. What does it mean, "We put on the breastplate of righteousness?" Friend, you employ the breastplate of righteousness by making a conscious commitment to bring your life into submission to Christ.

When tuning an instrument it is imperative that when a bandleader or conductor calls for the band to strike an "A" that they all have the same "A." Otherwise, the sound would be chaos. Around the year 1945, technology was a place where we could measure and determine exactly what define an "A." The tool used for measuring sound determined that an "A" represents 440 vibrations per minute. Not 430, not 450; 440 vibrations per minute always and forever equaled an "A."

If everything is tuned properly, it doesn't matter what the instrument is, when it attempts to produce an "A" note it should vibrate 440 times per minute because that is the standard for an "A" note.

As you live your life in concert with Christ, you will find that on a daily basis your life will fall out of tune. Putting on the breastplate of practical righteousness is tuning your life to CHRIST as the STANDARD.

3. The Shoes of Peace

Ephesians 6:15 " *and having shod YOUR FEET WITH THE PREPARATION OF THE GOSPEL OF PEACE—*" Paul's analogy comes from Isaiah 52:7 *"How lovely on the mountains are the feet of him who brings good news, Who announces peace and brings good news of happiness, Who announces salvation, and says to Zion, "Your God reigns!"* (emphasis mine)

Shoes of peace may seem odd upon a warrior. But, such is the nature of your battle. While we wage war on that which God wages war, Satan and demons; we come as ambassadors of God to our fellow man; calling them to make peace with Christ.

(Isaiah 1:18) *"Come now, and let us reason together," Says the LORD, "Though your sins are as scarlet, They will be as white as snow; Though they are red like crimson, They will be like wool."* (2 Corinthians 5:20) *"Therefore, we are ambassadors for Christ, as though God were making an appeal through us; we beg you on behalf of Christ, be reconciled to God."*

The Roman Soldiers Shoes were a sturdy pair of boots. A good pair of boots ensures a soldier will be ready to march, climb, fight or whatever else is necessary. Christ demands the same readiness of his people. (I Peter 3:15) *"...always being ready to make a defense to everyone who asks you to give an account for the hope that is in you, yet with gentleness and reverence-"*

What does it mean to wear the shoes of peace? Often times, we think about the shoes of peace as meaning we are to be arbitrators, peacemakers, which we are. (Matthew 5:9) *"Blessed are the peacemakers, for they shall be called sons of God."* There is an even greater application than that of a peacemaker.

Friend, more importantly, wearing these shoes means that when you enter into your day, you are looking for opportunities to bring people closer to Christ. Obviously, real peace can only come from having a relationship with Jesus.

When you sit down for lunch, are you thinking, "Where will my server spend eternity?" When you enter an elevator, do you ask yourself, "Why would the sovereign God of the universe allow me to be on an elevator with these people at this time?"

Wearing the shoes of peace should lead you to talk to your friends, your neighbors, your co-workers and family about having peace through salvation. The world shoves turmoil, fear, discontent, anger and rebellion in our face every day. Put on your "shoes" and show those walking with you how to find peace through the peacemaker.

Let's take a moment to evaluate our armor we have "put on" so far. Those first three pieces that we just discussed are the armor that soldiers commonly wear, belt, breastplate and shoes. The last three pieces of armor, the soldier takes up as he enters intense battle; the shield, the helmet and the sword.

4. The Shield of Faith

(Ephesians 6:16) *"—in addition to all, taking up the shield of faith with which you will be able to extinguish all the flaming arrows of the evil one."*

The Apostle Paul's analogy could have come from any one of a multitude of Old Testament passages. Here is only a small sampling of verses that could have been Paul's inspiration.

(Psalms 28:7) *The LORD is my strength and my shield; My heart trusts in Him, and I am helped; Therefore my heart exults, And with my song I shall thank Him.*

(Psalms18:2) *The LORD is my rock and my fortress and my deliverer, My God, my rock, in whom I take refuge; My shield and the horn of my salvation, my stronghold.*

(Genesis 15:1) *After these things the word of the LORD came to Abram in a vision, saying, "Do not fear, Abram, I am a shield to you; Your reward shall be very great."*

(Deuteronomy 33:29) *"Blessed are you, O Israel; Who is like you, a people saved by the LORD, Who is the shield of your help And the sword of your majesty! So your enemies will cringe before you, And you will tread upon their high places."*

(Psalm 33:20) *Our soul waits for the LORD; He is our help and our shield.*

(Psalm 84:11) *For the LORD God is a sun and shield; The LORD gives grace and glory; No good thing does He withhold from those who walk uprightly.*

God, Himself, is described as our, "shield"; how appropriate that our spiritual armor should include the shield that faith in God, Himself, represents. Now, let's learn a bit about the soldier's shield that he wears into battle so we can more clearly see how strong our Godly protection is.

The Roman Soldier's Shield

"The kind of shield Paul refers to here was the thureos. This shield was about two and half feet wide and four and a half feet high, designed to protect the entire body of the soldier, who was considerably smaller than the average man today.

The shield was made of a solid piece of wood and was covered with metal or heavy oiled leather. They normally stood side by side with their shields together, forming a huge phalanx extending as long as a mile or more.

The archers stood behind this protective wall of shields and shot their arrows as they advanced against the enemy. Anyone who stood or crouched behind such shields was protected from the barrage of enemy arrows and spears." (The MacArthur New Testament Commentary, Moody Publishers. The Shield of Faith)

The spiritual flaming missiles against which believers need protection would most often be temptation. Satan continually bombards God's children with temptation of immorality, hatred, envy, anger, covetousness, pride, doubt, fear, despair, distrust and every other sin you can ever think of.

Remember, God tempts no one, we are led aside by our own lusts. (James 1:13) *Let no one say when he is tempted, "I am being tempted by God" for God cannot be tempted by evil, and He Himself does not tempt anyone. 14 But each one is tempted when he is carried away and enticed by his own lust."* Satan knows our weaknesses and once we take the bait—the battle is ON.

However, first, before we talk about God's shield of faith, I want to make sure you know that you are not alone in your situation, no matter what it is.

(I Corinthians 10:13) *"No temptation has overtaken you but such as is common to man; and God is faithful, who will not allow you to be tempted beyond what you are able, but with the temptation will provide the way of escape also, so that you will be able to endure it."* You are not alone in your temptation or alone in your circumstances.

What does it mean to take up the shield of faith? Every moment of temptation there is what I call a "MOMENT OF CRISIS;" the defining moment when you have to decide whether you are going to fold or fight. Which way you go will have everything to do with whether or not you believe God's Word is a stronghold.

Let's think about a life situation where temptation is presented as a way out. You made a mistake; big or small, you made a poor choice. You may have already yielded to the first temptation, now you face another temptation because you yielded to the first temptation.

Confronted with the first mistake, you are tempted to lie about it and shift the blame to somebody else. God's Word says we should not lie; in your moment of crisis, you must decide to lift the shield of faith.

God will make a way for you, whether to make the mistake right or to work through the consequences. Don't make one sin into two. Confess your sins, He is faithful to forgive and help you to work through any circumstances that may have come from your original mistake.

Perhaps you have gotten into a difficult place in your marriage. Satan shoots an arrow of discouragement and doubt; "give up, cash it in, it's not worth the effort." Friend, there is always help, through God's Word and through Godly counsel by trusted Christ based counselors. Never be ashamed to seek help; shame is one of Satan's tools.

God has given us tools, weapons, to stave off the attacks of the evil one. The shield of faith is to hold in front of us to deflect the fiery arrows of temptation, discouragement, confusion and doubt. When you hide God's Word in your heart, you can draw on the strength, direction and wisdom for every life situation.

(Psalms 119:11 TLB) *I have thought much about your words and stored them in my heart so that they would hold me back from sin.*

5. The Helmet of Salvation.

(Ephesians 6:17) *"And take THE HELMET OF SALVATION, and the sword of the Spirit, which is the word of God." Paul once again makes an analogy from Isaiah, 59, where Yahweh the victorious warrior wears "the helmet of salvation."* Let's see what the purpose of wearing a helmet in battle is.

The Roman Soldier's Helmet: "The purpose of the helmet, of course, was to protect the head from injury, particularly from the dangerous broadsword commonly used in the warfare of that day. That was not the much smaller sword mentioned later in this verse but was a large two-handed, double-edged sword that measured three to four feet in length. It was often carried by cavalrymen, who would swing at the heads of enemy soldiers to split their skulls or decapitate them.

To discourage us he (Satan) points to our failures, our sins, our unresolved problems, our poor health, or to whatever else seems negative in our lives in order to make us lose confidence in the love and care of our heavenly Father." {The MacArthur New Testament Commentary, Moody Publishers. "The Helmet of Salvation"} (parentheses mine)

It has been said that, "The mind is the devil's playground." Thoughts of discouragement, doubts and failure are all tools of Satan. To cause us to doubt God's presence in our life Satan raises questions about what we've done, and not done. "Did you pray today? Did you pray the prayer correctly? Was your prayer made out of selfish motives or a pure heart? Is your heart really pure?"

The helmet of salvation moves the emphasis from our own doings to what Christ has done. Christianity doesn't shout, "Do!" It quietly whispers, "DONE." Our salvation is not about what we do but about what Christ did at Calvary.

What do you do to put on the helmet of salvation? You recognize the need for forgiveness. (Romans 3:23) *"for all have sinned and come short of the glory of God."*

You acknowledge that the price for your sin was paid on Calvary's cross when Jesus died. (Romans 5:8) *But God demonstrates His own love toward us, in that while we were yet sinners, Christ died for us.*

(Romans 9-10) *that if you confess with your mouth Jesus as Lord, and believe in your heart that God raised Him from the dead, you will be saved; 10 for with the heart a person believes, resulting in righteousness, and with the mouth he confesses, resulting in salvation.*

"That's all," you say? That's it, the devil works over time to make you think it's hard. This is where your new life in Christ starts. One more time, in a simple list:

1. Recognize your sin
2. Acknowledge the price Jesus paid was for you.
3. Confess your sin; ask for Christ's forgiveness.

Friend, I can't tell you how happy it makes me to welcome you to the Family. If you've already taken those steps, I rejoice in your fellowship with the body of believers. Now, let's get back to our study on the FULL armor of God.

6. The Sword of the Spirit.

(Ephesians 6:17b) *"and the sword of the Spirit, which is the Word of God."* The Greek word, sword, in Ephesians is "rhema," and it means the Word of God, spoken right now, as you need it.

Paul once again may have made an analogy from Isaiah, this time perhaps from chapter 19:15 *"From His mouth comes a sharp sword, so that with it He may strike down the nations."*

Let's take a look at the type of weapon that Paul used to describe the Sword of the Spirit. Paul referred to the "machaira," which was six to eighteen inches long. Roman foot soldiers often carried it; it was used in hand-to-hand combat.

The sword, carried in a sheath or scabbard, was worn on their belt so it was always easy to grab for use. Paul explicitly stated that the sword of the Spirit is the Word of God.

(Hebrews 4:12) *"For the word of God is living and active and sharper than any two-edged sword, and piercing as far as the division of soul and spirit, of both joints and marrow, and able to judge the thoughts and intentions of the heart."*

What a perfect analogy of the Word of God; always sharp, ready at hand, cutting asunder flesh from bone. I love the realization that the sins my flesh wants to hold on tight to are no match for the strength and power of God's Word.

When I have a sin that won't let go of my flesh—I find a scripture that fits my problem. I write it down and hold it close at hand so when that temptation rises, I can grab my "sword." Let's talk more about this mighty weapon.

What does it mean to take up the sword of the Spirit? It means that you learn, meditate on and proclaim the truth of God's Word in your everyday life. You respond to every lie with God's truth. You face every temptation with the Sword of the Spirit, God's Word.

Now that you know how powerful and effective your sword is—where do you keep it? The battle sword that Paul spoke of was kept on the soldier's belt, at the ready. Does this mean you should carry your Bible in your pocket?

Many do. Perhaps more should. However, in the face of temptation, there is rarely time to stop, pull out your "sword," and look up the applicable verse to face your foe. God's Word answers the question. (Psalms 119:11) *I have stored what you have said in my heart, so I won't sin against you. (ISV)*

Chapter 8

The Battle in the Home

One of my favorite things about being a Dad is the privilege of tucking my kinds into bed at night. A couple of years ago, I started laying my hand on my kids and saying a prayer of blessing and protection over them every night.

During those "Daddy and me" moments, where they have my full attention, they can ask the most profound questions.

"Dad, did Eve have a belly button?"

"Dad, what does God do for fun?"

"Dad, who does God pray to?"

Well, one night when I was tucking my oldest daughter in, she asked, "Dad, why does God let the devil exist? Why doesn't He just go on and throw the devil into Hell and get it over with?"

Two thoughts came to my own mind. #1. Why do you come up with questions like this when it is time for bed? And, #2. WOW, that really IS a good question.

In fact, number two is a great question, one that many people have asked and frankly, I'm not able to answer fully, at this time. I can tell you that Satan and demons are allowed to exist and even wreak a measure of havoc on humanity because it will ultimately bring great glory to God.

You may be thinking, "How can something bad bring glory to God?" Good question, so, where do we turn when we want answers about God; to His Word, of course.

(Romans 5:3-5) *Not only that, but we also boast in our sufferings, knowing that suffering produces endurance, 4 endurance produces character, and character produces hope. 5 Now this hope does not disappoint us, because God's love has been poured out into our hearts by the Holy Spirit, who has been given to us.*

In this life, it is unclear why God allows suffering. Many verses show that He DOES allow it and many that show good that came of suffering. Sometimes, we never know the reason, this side of heaven. We know that God is faithful. Not "faithful because." Not, "faithful when-." He IS faithful.

A verse that addresses the question about suffering best, in my humble opinion is, (I Corinthians 13:12) *"For now we see in a mirror dimly, but then face to face; now I know in part, but then I will know fully just as I also have been fully known."*

Our response to suffering depends much on how you personally respond to evil against you and the evil around you. Job, in the Old Testament, is well known for his suffering and, his response to it. God allowed Satan to attack Job because He knew that Job's ultimate response would be commitment to God. God knew Job, and had no fear that Job would give up.

The story unfolds, revealing the full range of human response. The story has many angles; first came Satan's challenge, then, God's assurance, Job's patience in suffering, the callous response of Job's friends to his suffering, and finally, the victorious conclusion. If you haven't read Job, I highly recommend it.

God allowed Satan to "sift Peter like wheat." (Luke 22:31-33) *"Simon, Simon, behold, Satan has demanded permission to sift you like wheat; 32 but I have prayed for you, that your faith may not fail; and you, when once you have turned again, strengthen your brothers." 33 But he said to Him, "Lord, with You I am ready to go both to prison and to death!"*

Make note that Peter's strength, when tested, failed, even though Peter was very self-confident. After the test, Peter did exactly what Jesus said he would do---went on to strengthen his brothers.

So, was Peter pre-destined to fail, before the test even started? No. God is omnipotent (all powerful), and omnipresent (everywhere at once.) There is a difference between predestination and foreknowledge. If I jump off the roof and you say, "You're going to break both your legs," you are not predestinating me for failure. You know the laws of gravity and you know I won't bounce.

God allowed Satan to send a thorn in the Apostle Paul's flesh, knowing it would humble Paul. I don't know if Paul thought he needed humbling before the thorn was applied, but God did.

Mel Gibson's character, Benjamin Martin, a war hero, in the movie, "The Patriot," said, "Make no mistake about it, this battle will not be fought on some distant shore, but in our own back yards." The battle against Satan isn't fought only on the pages of scripture or only in the world around us.

It is fought in your home, in your own family. Your children are not casualties of war; they are one of the primary targets. Demons plant seeds that they hope, will be harvested in the decimation of the young souls they try to cultivate.

The Bible tells of a Mother that knew what it was like for the battle to come to her own backyard. Matthew 15 and Mark 7 tell of the event that took place in the district of Tyre and Sidon. First, let's take a look at the region and times the scripture speaks of.

Today, we know the region as, Southern Lebanon; it was a distinctly Gentile region, far from the authority of Herod or the influence of the Pharisees. Why would Jesus go to this place?

Mark seems to suggest in his account of the occasion that perhaps Jesus was seeking to take a vacation of sorts.

(Mark 7:24a) *"Jesus got up and went away from there to the region of Tyre. And when He had entered a house, He wanted no one to know of it- "*

During this time, a woman approached Jesus, asking Him to heal her daughter. Two things need to be known so you understand Jesus' seemingly harsh response:

1. It was unseemly that a woman, alone, would speak to any man in that society.

2. The woman was a Greek (Gentile), Greek's were considered so unclean that even being in their presence could defile you. (John 18:28) 28 Then they led Jesus from Caiaphas into the Praetorium (governor's house), and it was early; and they themselves did not enter into the Praetorium so that they would not be defiled, but might eat the Passover. (Parentheses mine)

Now, let's read about the incident in Mark.

(Mark 7:25-30) *"But after hearing of Him, a woman whose little daughter had an unclean spirit immediately came and fell at His feet. 26 Now the woman was a Gentile, of the Syrophoenician race. And she kept asking Him to cast the demon out of her daughter. 27 And He was saying to her, "Let the children be satisfied first, for it is not good to take the children's bread and throw it to the dogs."*

28 But she answered and said to Him, "Yes, Lord, but even the dogs under the table feed on the children's crumbs." 29 And He said to her, "Because of this answer go; the demon has gone out of your daughter." 30 And going back to her home, she found the child lying on the bed, the demon having left."

That event brings up a serious question in a parent's mind. Can children be attacked and oppressed by demons?

The scripture suggests that yes, they can. I would say they are particularly vulnerable; that is why Dad's need to be very careful to lead their homes in Christ. Don't allow compromise to open the door for demonic influence in your home. Nothing is sadder than seeing a child under the influence of demonic spirits.

I had been speaking on consecutive nights at a Church in which God was doing a great work, both during and after my arrival. During our first service, a Mother in her thirties was saved. After a few days, the mother brought her young boy to me and said, "I don't know what's wrong with my son, but it's really scaring me."

She told me she had never heard the boy use profanity until the night after she came to Christ. On the way home from Church, she turned the car radio to a Christian music station. The boy, only 5 years old, yelled out a string of profanity and demanded that she turn off the radio.

The second night at Church a picture of the cross was projected on the overhead screens behind the stage. When the boy saw the cross, he became agitated and said that he saw the devil with the cross. He was clearly hallucinating.

After the third night of these same sorts of occurrences, the mother brought the boy to me. I prayed over him and instructed the mother to discipline the child as she would anytime when he behaved in such a way.

Along with the discipline, I instructed her to teach her son about Christ and the Gospel. Instances like this one and many others remind us that our children are not off limits to the influence of evil. Instead, they are on the front lines of the battlefield.

As a Christian, I'm sure you're asking yourself why God would allow Satan to attack a child. I think the answer is found in the development of the mother's (parent's) faith. Notice how it was the mother's newly found and growing faith that seemed to lead to the child's odd behavior.

Let's look again at the woman in Mark 7 experience. Scripture says she was a Canaanite woman. As such, she was likely raised in a pagan culture that had been renowned for its wickedness and vile behaviors.

She was a descendant of a people God had commanded Israel to conquer and "utterly destroy." (Deuteronomy 7: 1-2) *"When the LORD your God brings you into the land where you are entering to possess it, and clears away many nations before you, the Hittites and the Girgashites and the Amorites and the Canaanites* and the Perizzites and the Hivites and the Jebusites, seven nations greater and stronger than you, 2 and when the LORD your God delivers them before you and you defeat them, then you shall utterly destroy them. You shall make no covenant with them and show no favor to them."

The Canaanite mother was probably a worshiper of Ashterath, the most popular deity of that region. I remind you that the Bible teaches Idol worship is actually demon worship. Paul warned the Church at Corinth of this reality in I Corinthians 10:20-21 "No, but I say that the things which the Gentiles sacrifice, they sacrifice to demons and not to God; and I do not want you to become sharers in demons. 21 You cannot drink the cup of the Lord and the cup of demons; you cannot partake of the table of the Lord and the table of demons."

Because Ashterath was a goddess of fertility, depictions of "her" often included children. The sacrifice of the first-born child frequently was made to "her." You may wonder how a child can become demon possessed; easily, because children were a focal part of the demon worship.

Consequently, this little girl may have become demon possessed through her mother's idolatry. The scripture doesn't go into great detail, but possibly, the mother was disillusioned, even frightened by what she had seen. She probably felt guilt in what her actions had caused to happen to her child.

The book of Mark tells us she had heard about Jesus and had gone out to meet him. Don't you love that? This mother was concerned about her baby; then something happened, something the demons didn't expect.

The mother found out about Jesus. Can you imagine how that mother felt the moment she heard the Good News that Jesus, the miracle worker, was nearby? Perhaps, she was washing clothes and a friend near her said, "Have you heard about this man they call, Jesus? They say he can work miracles and even calm the storm."

Another friend could have added, "They say he can feed the multitudes. They say the winds and the sea obey him. They say he has authority over demons!"

Can you imagine how that young mother's heart may have leapt in hopeful anticipation? OH, those demons had not planned on the mother getting that news! That, my friend, was GOOD NEWS.

Jim Croce wrote a song about a poolroom hustler who hustled the wrong fellow. The key verse to the song said, "You don't tug on Superman's Cape, you don't spit in the wind, you don't pull the mask off the Lone Ranger, and you don't mess around with Slim!" Well, that demon would learn all too well that you don't mess around with a Mother who knows how to go after Jesus.

That Canaanite Mother found Jesus and began to cry out, saying, "Have mercy on me, Lord, Son of David, my daughter is cruelly demon-possessed!" Interesting that she addresses Jesus as the Jewish Messiah, "Lord, Son of David."

Notice that even though she addressed Jesus as the Messiah for another people and another land, He did respond to her, shortly. (Matthew 15:23-24) *But He did not answer her a word. And His disciples came and implored Him, saying, "Send her away, because she keeps shouting at us." 24 But He answered and said, "I was sent only to the lost sheep of the house of Israel."*

It's as if Jesus was saying, "You said it yourself, I am the Son of David. I am their Messiah." The mother was not swayed, addressing Jesus as a Messiah wasn't enough. Addressing him as THE Messiah was not enough. The Mother pressed in, unhindered by the abrupt dismissal.

Boldly, she stood her ground. (Matthew 15:25) *But she came and began to bow down before Him, saying, "Lord, help me!"* (Emphasis mine) Now, she had moved passed "their" Messiah and addressed Jesus as HER Messiah, saying, "LORD-." When she called out to Jesus for her own sake, she was saying, "Jesus, right now, this minute, you are not just one worthy of the Hebrews worship or Humanities Worship, you are one worthy of MY worship."

The Disciples tried to discourage the mother, (Matthew 23b) -- *And His disciples came and implored Him, saying, "Send her away, because she keeps shouting at us."* Jesus had dismissed her, yet she kept insisting that he help her.

Right here, I want to say something; it is OK to get emotional on behalf of your baby, your children. That's a problem in our country today, we rarely see moms and dads broken when their child begins to rebel, influenced by the devil.

In fact, too often, parents actually do things for and with their children to encourage their spiritual decline. The desires, fashions and pastimes of the world should not be brought into a Christ centered home.

Parents, your praying and tears can do what a youth minister can't, what a school system won't. Scripture says (James 5:16) *Therefore, confess your sins to one another, and pray for one another so that you may be healed. The effective prayer of a righteous man can accomplish much.*

Anne Graham Lotz told a couple to lay the shoes of their rebellious daughter on the altar and pray that her feet would be moved to repentance. I believe we need to get to the place where it is a regular occurrence to see parents crying out to God on behalf of their children.

Too often parents wait to pray fervent prayers until rebellion sets in. Committed prayer should be made from the moment of conception throughout their formative years and on into adulthood. Prayer should not be a last resort; it should be an on-going, part of your life-style.

Back to the study at hand, the Canaanite woman pleading with Christ to heal her daughter. Can you see the development of her faith? She had worshipped Asterath and now, her daughter was demon possessed. The Mother hears about Jesus and goes to seek Him out in the market place where she'd heard He was.

Let's stop again for a moment; I have to wonder, where is the DADDY? Maybe he was golfing, working, fishing, I don't know what men did back then for leisure activity. Wherever he was, if he was present in the home, why wasn't he with Mom, crying out to Jesus?

Steve Hale, a well known evangelist from Woodstock, GA, researched the effect an absent Father has on a family. His findings were revealing.

\# 70% of America's adolescent murderers, long term prisoners and teenage runaways come from fatherless homes.

\# Those children without a father are five times more likely to live in poverty, four times more likely to have behavioral problems that require psychiatric treatment, twice as likely to drop out of school and twice as likely to go to jail.

\# A study of 39 teenaged girls who were suffering from anorexia showed that 36 of them lacked a close relationship with their father.

\# A John's Hopkins University study found that young white teenage girls living in fatherless homes were 60% more likely to have premarital sex than those living in two parent homes.

In 25 years of working in prisons, Bill Glass (famous football player elected to The Football Hall of Fame in 1985, author of "Get in the Game," and minister at Bill Glass Ministries well known for his work in prisons) testifies that he has never met a prisoner who loved their Dad.

Most of the world's renowned atheists come from father-less homes.

The active presence of a Father in the home is extremely important. However, I also know that a mom that's willing to pour her heart out to Jesus can raise Christ centered children. Steven Brogli, a friend from my first pastorate, is leading student ministry. He is reaching record numbers of souls for Christ; a Godly single Mother raised him.

Let's focus once again on the Canaanite woman who was wanting Jesus to heal her daughter. She didn't give up, after the Lord told her to leave, she leaned in even closer; Calling him, "Lord." (Matthew 15:23) *But He did not answer her a word.*

Does that moment fit what you know of Jesus? Dr. Robert Smith Jr., Dean of Christian Preaching who holds the Charles T. Carter Baptist Chair of Divinity at Beeson Divinity School, Samford University, spoke of our current view of the Christ this way. "I am afraid the Church is committing Christological Idolatry.

Worshipping a Christ that immediately acts, who immediately comforts and speaks. People today often want a cosmic vending machine that they can walk up to, put in their quarter and get what they want. When they don't get what they want, they protest. But more often than not, Jesus doesn't act as we think He ought."

Most often, Christianity doesn't fit into simple equations of unenlightened human reason. From time to time, Jesus shocks us with His Words or His ways. Be patient with me, please. I realize I'm going back and forth here, but there is an important truth for us in the telling of this event. SO MUCH information, to digest, hang with me, we're almost there.

The disciples not only avoided the woman, they were downright rude, *"23b Send her away because she keeps shouting at us--."* Even Jesus himself told her he wasn't there for her people, *"24 I was sent only to the lost sheep of Israel."* But the Momma was desperate, her baby girl was suffering and it could be all because she, the Mom, had been worshipping idols.

After the Disciples derided her and Jesus rebuked her, what did that Mom do? She pressed in harder. Make note that as the woman's faith grew, so did her passionate seeking. She bowed down before Jesus, and cried out, "25b Lord, help me!"

Jesus' response, *"26b It is not good to take the children's bread and throw it to the dogs."* Did you see that? Jesus called her a dog. Can you imagine? Jesus would have flunked all the church growth courses! We look at that and wonder what on earth was going on.

Several commentators have tried their best to take up for Jesus saying that he wasn't referring to a mongrel or a street dog. Surely, he must have been comparing her to a domesticated, pure bread or at least a cute little house dog.

I don't care if somebody calls you a dingo or a Chihuahua, they are still calling you a dog. What would you do if Jesus called you a dog? Would you cry? Would you back up and be offended? Well Jesus did and the woman didn't.

She kept right on pressing in. Have you ever been insulted but were left speechless until hours later? Long after the insult, you think, "I should have said --." This mom didn't have that problem.

The Bible doesn't say, but I think by this time, Mom had tears streaming, dirt had soiled her clothing and her face. She'd been pushed, shoved and maybe even trampled. Every bone must have ached with her struggle to convince the man, Jesus, the one who had been seen casting out demons, to intervene for her daughter.

Even in what must have been a horrible, emotionally anguished state, Mom did not suffer from a loss of comeback words. *27 But she said, "Yes, Lord; but even the dogs feed on the crumbs which fall from their masters' table."*

WOW, I'm not sure I could think of a comeback like that ever, much less as an immediate response. (Matthew 15: 28) *Then Jesus said to her, "O woman, your faith is great; it shall be done for you as you wish." And her daughter was healed at once.*

God used that horrible situation to point the Mother away from idol worship to Jesus. God didn't want that woman's daughter to be demon possessed. Much like what happens today, our children reflect their upbringing. The choices we make hold consequences for not only our lives, but also the lives of those around us, particularly, our children.

Do your children live in the safety net of knowing that they have parents faithfully seeking Jesus on their behalf? They should. If they can't, you need to fix that. Now, here, finally, is the place I've been bringing you to; a place of realization. God desires the same thing for you as He desired for the Canaanite woman, that you would lay aside your idols and turn to Christ. An "idol" is anything, or person, that you put before your love for Jesus.

Is your life full of conflict; is your marriage in trouble? Is there something missing in your life? Seek Christ. Is your child under the influence of demons? Seek Christ. Regardless of your life circumstances, or your current spiritual situation, whether saved, lost, hot, cold, lukewarm--- SEEK CHRIST. (Proverbs 8:17) *"I love those who love me; And those who diligently seek me will find me."*

Chapter 9
Prayer and Spiritual Warfare

(Ephesians 1:16-19) *I do not cease to give thanks for you, remembering you in my prayers, 17 that the God of our Lord Jesus Christ, the Father of glory, may give you the Spirit of wisdom and of revelation in the knowledge of him, 18 having the eyes of your hearts enlightened, that you may know what is the hope to which he has called you, what are the riches of his glorious inheritance in the saints, 19 and what is the immeasurable greatness of his power toward us who believe, according to the working of his great might*

(Ephesians:14-19) *For this reason I bow my knees before the Father, 15 from whom every family in heaven and on earth is named, 16 that according to the riches of his glory he may grant you to be strengthened with power through his Spirit in your inner being, 17 so that Christ may dwell in your hearts through faith—that you, being rooted and grounded in love, 18 may have strength to comprehend with all the saints what is the breadth and length and height and depth, 19 and to know the love of Christ that surpasses knowledge, that you may be filled with all the fullness of God.*

In Paul's letter to the Ephesians, Paul calls us to personally, regularly engage in prayer. Paul was intimately aware that prayer is not always a scheduled activity nor is it a high, lofty speech fabricated to impress listeners. Prayer isn't a tool to get what you want, when you want it, as if God is a big Santa in the sky. Nor is prayer a monologue; it is a dialogue, a conversation. Conversation is a vital part of any relationship.

Prayer is having a conversation with God. If you only talked to your spouse when you needed something, what kind of relationship would you have? It certainly would not be a close relationship, for sure. Let's look at how relationship and our faith grow through prayer.

To start with, I need to make a confession to you. In my early walk with God, I never liked sermons on prayer. I knew how to pray, I tried to find time to pray every day. As I grew in Christ, I discovered prayer isn't something I do, it's about a relationship I have.

Sometimes, the reason we don't pray is the same reason we don't run. When I first interviewed at a church where I was invited to join the staff, I met Mike Yarnell. He had noticed on my resume that I had listed one of my hobbies as running.

So that you can know the background of my running "hobby," you need to know that I spent months getting ready to run a 5k; a race that I barely finished. So, when I said I considered running a hobby, I used the term very loosely.

Back to my first meeting with Mr. Yarnell; he said, "So you are a runner, huh?" I said, "Yeah, I'm a runner." He said, "You want to run with me sometime?"

(Me) "Sure, how far you go?"

(Mr. Yarnell) "I try to put in a 5K every day at lunch."

I could have swallowed hard, and accepted the challenge. In time, with commitment, I could have made my "hobby," into a healthy commitment to my lifestyle. However, instead, that day marked the retirement of my running career, not my commitment. Mark this "choice" in your memory; I will bring it up again later.

Every book I ever read and every sermon I have ever heard on prayer was filled with illustration after illustration of men who "ran marathons" in prayer. Martin Luther was in the habit of praying four hours per day, except when he was busy. Then he prayed more.

Well, while some of us are marathon runners and some of us can pray for hours every day, most of us are normal folk that need to exercise more and really need to engage in prayer more often. So here's what I'm going to do, I'm going to do what I believe the Word does. I'm going to give you encouragement and motivation to pray.

I made an acrostic, a word puzzle where every letter stands for a word that represents another word. Acrostics can make an instruction or procedure easier to remember and commonly are used in the medical field, industry and education systems.

ACTS Each letter makes a memory point

\#   A Adoration

\#   C Confession

\#   T Thanksgiving

\#   S Supplication

You know that prayer is a conversation with God and now you have a memory tool for the steps taken in prayer. So, how do we start this conversation? Do you remember when you first met your best friend? You shuffled your feet, mumbled some introductory phrases, exchanged pleasantries and then—said, "Hey, nice meeting you, um, bye." In time, a relationship grew.

Prayer isn't or at least, doesn't have to be, like that. God created you; He has a plan for your life. He knows every thought you ever had, every act you ever did and every word you've ever spoken. Imagine a relationship where you don't have to be concerned with saying the wrong thing, or messing up what you are trying to say. No matter what you say, it won't surprise God.

AND, He genuinely cares about everything in your life. Even though He is aware of every moment you've lived, He loves to hear you tell Him about it. We (mankind) were created for companionship. In the beginning, before Adam and Eve made a bad choice, scripture suggests that God would meet with them in the Garden in the cool of the evening.

(Genesis 3:8) *And they heard the sound of the LORD God walking in the garden in the cool of the day, and the man and his wife hid themselves from the presence of the LORD God among the trees of the garden.*

This scripture is often used as proof of God's keeping fellowship with Adam and Eve. However, make note that this "walking" was only mentioned AFTER the sin had been done. However, I choose to think the evening walk was a usual event. The verse doesn't say Adam yelled, "OH no, here comes GOD! We're in trouble now! HIDE!"

The simple statement that God was walking in the cool of the evening, in the garden sounds more like, there is an understood, "like He always did." All that aside, I'm choosing to go with the idea that God had fellowship with his people. Sometimes I wonder what they talked about, probably everyday stuff.

Sin is what had separated us from God, when Adam and Eve CHOSE to do what seemed good to them instead of what God had instructed them to do, the relationship between God and His creation, mankind, was broken.

When Jesus died at Calvary, He paid the eternal price for all sin, your sin, my sin, the sin of the world. The payment of that sin healed the rift and relationship was restored.

(Hebrews 4:16) *Let us then approach God's throne of grace with confidence (BOLDLY), so that we may receive mercy and find grace to help us in our time of need.* (parenthesis mine)

Yes, He is the Almighty God, the Lord of Lords, King of Kings, Master of the Universe, creator of all that is, ever was and ever will be. There is no thing too difficult for Him. No issue in your life or mine that He isn't intimately aware of.

So, how do you talk to such a super being? The same way the President's child talks to their Dad. Though there is an awareness of the prestige and positon, an intimacy exists because of relationship.

Let's take a moment to review our own personal relationship with God. Rather than explain it all, I'm going to let the Word speak. The whole book of Romans is an EXCELLENT study. The Apostle Paul is said to have written this letter to the churches in Rome on one of his trips to Corinth.

From that letter comes the "Roman Road" path to salvation; often used as an evangelistic tool. Read these scriptures, if you know them, review one more time; because, well, it's always good.

(Romans 3:23-24) --*for all have sinned and fall short of the glory of God, 24 and are justified by his grace as a gift, through the redemption that is in Christ Jesus—*

(Romans 6:23) *For the wages of sin is death, but the free gift of God is eternal life in Christ Jesus our Lord.*

(Romans 10:9) -- *because, if you confess with your mouth that Jesus is Lord and believe in your heart that God raised him from the dead, you will be saved.*

Here's another acronym that explains how to begin a relationship with Jesus. Do you notice that both acronyms I've used spell out ACT? Like any relationship, there is input from BOTH sides. Relationship requires a dialog, not a monologue; speak, listen.

A Acknowledge that you are a sinner
C Confess your sin and accept forgiveness
T Tell somebody about your new relationship

The question we need to address is how do we find motivation to take the time to pray? I believe that there are both motivations and hindrances to prayer.

The strongest motivation for prayer is probably imminent danger. If the roof suddenly started caving in, you and everybody else in the building would feel the need for fervent, immediate, even dramatic—prayer. You would no longer have fear of being mocked or pointed out.

No thought would be given to decorum or manners or how to pray effectively. Indeed, in one accord EVERYbody would begin to cry out to God with great expression and fervor. Nobody would be looking around to see how everybody else was praying.

Without a clear and present danger, if the Pastor called the body of Christ to pray there'd be shuffling of feet, clearing of throats, maybe a few mumbles and a lot of silence; um, I mean silent prayer-of course. I can pretty much guarantee the only fervent thought going on would be, "Ok, how long to pray is long enough?"

If the congregation was asked to gather in groups of five to pray, there would be seeking out of close friends so there would be less fear of our prayer habits being examined. There'd be mumbling about it being "cold and flu season," so we shouldn't stand—too close, and thoughts to "what time is it, anyway?"

In the Garden of Gethsemane Jesus was praying so hard, with such deep emotion that he began to sweat drops of blood. Meantime, the disciples were sleeping nearby, unmoved to join in the time of prayer.

(Matthew 26:36-44) *Then Jesus went with them to a place called Gethsemane, and he said to his disciples, "Sit here, while I go over there and pray." 37 And taking with him Peter and the two sons of Zebedee, he began to be sorrowful and troubled. 38 Then he said to them, "My soul is very sorrowful, even to death; remain here, and watch with me." 39 And going a little farther he fell on his face and prayed, saying, "My Father, if it be possible, let this cup pass from me; nevertheless, not as I will, but as you will."*

38 Then he said to them, "My soul is very sorrowful, even to death; remain here, and watch with me." 39 And going a little farther he fell on his face and prayed, saying, "My Father, if it be possible, let this cup pass from me; nevertheless, not as I will, but as you will."

40 And he came to the disciples and found them sleeping. And he said to Peter, "So, could you not watch with me one hour? 41 Watch and pray that you may not enter into temptation. The spirit indeed is willing, but the flesh is weak."

42 Again, for the second time, he went away and prayed, "My Father, if this cannot pass unless I drink it, your will be done." 43 And again he came and found them sleeping, for their eyes were heavy. 44 So, leaving them again, he went away and prayed for the third time, saying the same words again.

What was the difference between Jesus' desire to be in prayer and his disciple's desire? The Christ knew what was coming. Once prayer was finished, the plan of the crucifixion would begin to play out. If the disciples had known what was about to happen, the events that were unfolding, they probably would have been stretched out on the grass beside their Lord, anguishing in prayer. However, they felt no such motivation and soon fell asleep. They had no sense of imminent danger.

When I was flying back from Guatemala to the New Orleans' Airport, there was a young lady sitting beside me who was a veterinarian. We talked about her career and my mission trip. It was soon obvious that she was much more interested in saving dogs than saving souls. I'm guessing from our conversation, she was an agnostic.

As the plane began its descent into the New Orleans' airport, a storm had gathered and we began to experience severe turbulence. There was lighting, thunder, and suddenly the plane dropped fifteen feet in altitude. Believe me, without thought to appearances or decorum, everybody in that plane, including the young woman who seemed to have no interest in any type of faith in anything---began to pray. Why? Danger.

The question is how do I keep a sense of urgency in prayer, without having the prompt of, "fear?" In Ephesians Chapter Six, Paul believes that the people have been listening to him and following his directions. He concludes in (Ephesians 6:10-15) *"10 Finally, be strong in the Lord and in the strength of his might. 11 Put on the whole armor of God, that you may be able to stand against the schemes of the devil. 12 For we do not wrestle against flesh and blood, but against the rulers, against the authorities, against the cosmic powers over this present darkness, against the spiritual forces of evil in the heavenly places.*

13 Therefore take up the whole armor of God, that you may be able to withstand in the evil day, and having done all, to stand firm. 14 Stand therefore, having fastened on the belt of truth, and having put on the breastplate of righteousness, 15 and, as shoes for your feet, having put on the readiness given by the gospel of peace."

Paul was personally aware, from his own experiences and the experiences of his fellow Christians, that following Christ means we <u>will</u> be engaging in spiritual warfare. The Devil and his demons want total destruction for your life. As his friend and fellow Disciple, Peter, said, (I Peter 5:8) *"Be sober-minded; be watchful. Your adversary the devil prowls around like a roaring lion, seeking someone to devour."*

Satan's goal is our total destruction and his plan is to set you up for failure so that you lose your moral witness through compromise and sin. The Apostle Paul told the Ephesians (Christians today should heed the same advice) that we MUST take up the full armor of God.

The temptations you face, whether your "demon" is pornography, drug abuse, bitterness, anger, ANYthing, person, activity or attitude that is not pleasing to God must be recognized as a weapon the enemy has formed to make YOU be ineffective and in time, fall.

Statistics reveal that a person over the age of 30 has most likely been exposed to pornography by the age of 12. Persons today younger than the age of 20 were most likely exposed to pornography by the age of 5. The age of exposure is getting younger and younger.

Remember at the start of this chapter, I told you to remember I'd made a choice to not develop my running hobby? Every day we must make a choice to develop the habits of living for Christ—or not. The choice not to run was an "I want an easier way to exercise," choice. The choice to follow Christ starts with prayer. A committed prayer life is simply making time in the busyness of life to talk to God. There is no "easier way," it IS that simple.

To grow and be fruitful in your Christ walk, to resist temptation, you must daily make the choice to spend time in prayer. Conversation is a vital part of relationship. A friend of mine fixes a cup of coffee, sits in a quiet place and talks to God as if He's sitting across the coffee table from her. She first acknowledges her Lord's presence, giving thanks and worship.

Worship is not a learned activity. It is an act of intimacy. The only way you can truly worship is to know God personally. Then worship is spontaneous, a response, not a responsibility.

We've given our life to Christ, now what do we do to develop an intimacy in prayer? First, let's look at some hindrances to prayer. Unbelievably, boredom can be a hindrance to prayer. Not God's boredom, He delights to hear you speak. Your boredom with the activity, the everyday "doing it," can be a problem.

Some people enjoy the consistency of a specific time and place for daily conversation with the Lord. They like a daily meeting with a friend, at an arranged time. The truth is, our personal life style and personality determine how we pray.

Typically, we pray the way we have heard someone else pray. My Pastor used to pray in King James English. Consequently, when I got saved, I spoke in everyday language but switched to King James when I'd pray. Why? Because that is the example that had been set for me.

Rev. Charles Spurgeon (June 1834-January 1892 a strong influence in the Reformed Baptist tradition) told of a young man's prayer in preaching school. The young man had gone to great pains to write out his prayer with the most precise and impressive of theological terms.

After the young preacher had eloquently prayed for quite some time, Rev. Spurgeon went to the podium. With kind advice, the great man said, "Son, call him Father and ask him for something."

Often, when we pray, we repeat Christianese words. Words that are common inside the church but don't necessarily mean anything. An example is the word, "bless." How many times do we pray, "bless (name)?" What does that mean?

The first definition given for "bless" in the dictionary is, "pronounce words in a religious rite." I make note that a slightly more in depth definition is given after that, "to invoke God's favor on." Still the most common meaning is simply, to say words in a ceremony.

Do we mean to bless with healing, knowledge, wisdom, strength, talent or an extra dip of ice-cream at the soda fountain? Are our prayers a ceremony, repeated daily to fulfill our Christian responsibility? We are to converse, to talk, to share, not--- participate in a ceremony. Prayer is a dialogue, not a monologue.

A few years ago, I challenged the men at our church to not nonchalantly say, "bless" while praying. Many reported that they couldn't even pray when the all-inclusive, benign "bless" was removed from their prayer vocabulary.

Prayer is a conversation, an intimate verbal and mental exchange between God and "me." Please note that I do NOT think that saying, "bless" is a bad thing. We just need to be aware of what we are saying instead of using an often non-descript word over and over.

Chapter 10
Prayer: What Why When & How

We are to approach God through prayer with reverence, but also in a natural conversation. It is not necessary to use big theological words; unless of course, you normally speak in those terms.

<u>Prayer is a conversation.</u>
Ephesians 6:18 says, *"And pray in the Spirit on all occasions with all kinds of prayers and requests. With this in mind, be alert and always keep on praying for all the Lord's people."*

There are five TYPES of prayer, adoration, petition, penitence, intercession and thanksgiving. Prayers of petition, penitence and intercession are all prayers that are "asking" for something; aieto, a Greek word that means, "a request with increasing urgency."

There are also specific activities of prayer.

\#   <u>Silence</u>. This is when we acknowledge God's presence; sit at His feet and our heart listens. This is a part of God's side of the prayer dialogue.

\#   <u>Praying through the scriptures</u>. We memorize verses, hiding them in our heart to encourage us. Pray those scriptures as part of your prayers; not because God needs reminded of the promises in His Word. Rather it is a reminder to us, ME, of His Word and His Sovereignty.

\#   <u>Fasting.</u> This is when, by God's divine direction, a congregational instruction in preparation for a specific ministry activity or event, or by our own desire to seek God's face in a deeper way, we do not eat. In a long fast, water and or juice is sometimes permitted, but not always.

Sometimes, in particularly long fasts or fasts done by persons who are medically restricted from a total fast, certain favorite foods are not eaten as a fast unto the Lord rather than the denial of all foods. Does fasting change God's mind? No. Fasting will change MY heart, bringing me the peace to accept and the humility to submit to God's sovereignty.

Let's remember that Paul's instruction was to pray "with all kinds of prayer." We are to pray in silence, constantly.

(I Thessalonians 5:16-18) *Rejoice always, pray without ceasing, give thanks in all circumstances; for this is the will of God in Christ Jesus for you.*

Nehemiah prayed as he was talking to the King (Nehemiah 2:4-5) *Then the king said to me, "What are you requesting?" So I prayed to the God of heaven. 5 And I said to the king, "If it pleases the king, and if your servant has found favor in your sight, that you send me to Judah, to the city of my fathers' graves, that I may rebuild it."*

Even in the pain of Godly discipline, scripture shows God's children whispered their penitent prayers.

(Isaiah 26:16) *O LORD, in distress they sought you; they poured out a whispered prayer when your discipline was upon them.*

We are to cry out in prayer as the Children of Israel did when they were held captive in Egypt,

(Exodus 2:23) *Now it came about in the course of those many days that the king of Egypt died. And the sons of Israel sighed because of the bondage, and they cried out; and their cry for help because of their bondage rose up to God.*

Jesus cried out in prayer in the Garden at Gethsemane (Matthew 27:46) *About the ninth hour Jesus cried out with a loud voice, saying, "ELI, ELI, LAMA SABACHTHANI?" that is, "MY GOD, MY GOD, WHY HAVE YOU FORSAKEN ME?"* (Emphasis mine)

When Do We Pray?

We should pray all the time, according to the scripture, alongside rejoicing and thanksgiving. (I Thessalonians 5:16-18) *Rejoice always, 17 pray without ceasing, 18 give thanks in all circumstances; for this is the will of God in Christ Jesus for you.*

Notably, this continuous prayer should be an attitude since we can't walk, drive or work with our eyes shut. As you move through the day, pray for people around you. First, pray that the Holy Spirit draw people to Christ. After prayer for salvation, every single person has a need, you don't know what their issue is, but God does.

The young couple beside you in the elevator may have terrible financial problems. The man at the coffee shop may have lost his job. The teenager in the car beside you at the traffic light white knuckling the steering wheel could be so broken they are contemplating suicide.

While you wait for the traffic light to change, ride in the elevator, and walk through the parking lot, pray. Heads up, it is during these silent prayers that the prayer can get—personal. Along with generalized prayer, ask that the Spirit would open your eyes to see opportunity to meet somebody's need. One of the blessings of continuous prayer is to be available to be God's hands.

As well as being prayerfully available, there is a time of prayer. In our busy lifestyles, how do we find time for committed prayer? The same way we find time to plan meetings, appointments and daily activities. The next question would obviously be; how do I keep that commitment? Again, the same way we keep our hair appointments, rotate our tires, show up for choir and any other important frequent life event.

When we view our relationship with God as having the same importance as our worldly schedules, we find it a natural part of life to have intimacy with God. Satan hates this commitment that leads to intimacy. In fact, right now, as you read the previous comment, you began to think about how difficult, perhaps even silly the idea of a committed prayer life is.

Recognize where that disparaging thought is coming from, and stop listening. Think back to the discussion about the helmet of salvation. The helmet covers our head, our ears and our mind. Adjust your helmet and turn attention to your committed relationship with your Lord.

A template for prayer

Maybe you are a person who can think on the move. You sit down for your prayer time and boom, you are in chat mode; the words start rolling.

I'm not like that. No matter who I'm talking to or what I'm doing, my mind builds a template to work from. The Lord's Prayer is usually my "go to" template; not always, but often.

The disciples asked Jesus how to pray.
(Matthew 6:9-20)

Pray then like this: "Our Father in heaven, hallowed be your name. 10 Your kingdom come, your will be done, on earth as it is in heaven. 11 Give us this day our daily bread, 12 and forgive us our debts, as we also have forgiven our debtors. 13 And lead us not into temptation, but deliver us from evil. 14 For if you forgive others their trespasses, your heavenly Father will also forgive you, 15 but if you do not forgive others their trespasses neither will your Father forgive your trespasses.

Make note that Jesus told them HOW to pray, not WHAT to pray. Using the Lord's response as my template, I add my own praise, requests thanksgiving and conversation.

"Our Father in heaven, hallowed be your name."

"My father in heaven, I honor you. You are the King of Kings, the Lord of Lords. You know the stars by name and the mountains tremble when you speak." (of course, choose your own words of recognition of the Almighty God)

Praise is a spontaneous response to an intimate knowledge. God doesn't need to be praised, intimacy makes us aware of the praise He is worthy of, like my mouth drools thinking of cake, my heart can't help but praise my God.

"Your kingdom come, your will be done, on earth as it is in heaven."

That verse is my "prompt" to pray for our government leaders, public officials, the safety of our first responders, and the moral fiber of our society. I call out the names of those I know in these positions.

Also included under this prompt are those I know who need Jesus, that they would be saved. I also pray that I would be aware and responsive to the prompting of the Holy Spirit to witness to those around me.

"Give us this day our daily bread, and forgive us our debts, as we also have forgiven our debtors."

My response is to thank God for the many blessings He has given me, a home, food to eat, a family that loves me—so many blessings. I ask God for a humble heart so that I'm aware of sin and quick to seek forgiveness. Anybody I have an issue with, I call out their name and ask God to help me to forgive them, to love them as Jesus loves.

"And lead us not into temptation, but deliver us from evil."

I respond with confessing to myself what my own sin weaknesses are and asking God to keep me from those things where I'm weak. In addition, at this point in my prayer conversation, I remind myself of 2 Corinthians 12:9 *But he said to me, "My grace is sufficient for you, for my power is made perfect in weakness." Therefore I will boast all the more gladly about my weaknesses, so that Christ's power may rest on me."* God's GOT this! I AM strong.

Again, this is the template that I most often use for prayer; it doesn't have to be yours. Use your own way of conversation. The important thing is, PRAY. Your Lord delights in hearing you tell what is in your heart, on your mind. Fancy words aren't necessary, unless of course, you talk that way in every day conversation. The thing is: be YOU.

Chapter 11

How Long Before God Answers My Prayers?

Now, we've talked about why we pray, what prayer is, when it should be made and how to pray. Finally, let's talk about how long do we have to pray before God answers? The "Shepherd King" David, a man after God's own heart, wondered the same thing. Who knew people thousands of years ago had the same issues we do? Time, circumstances and governments change, but the sinful heart of man and the faithfulness of God is constant.

(Psalms 13) *To the choirmaster. A Psalm of David.*
13 How long, O LORD? Will you forget me forever? How long will you hide your face from me? 2 How long must I take counsel in my soul and have sorrow in my heart all the day? How long shall my enemy be exalted over me?

3 Consider and answer me, O LORD my God; light up my eyes, lest I sleep the sleep of death, 4 lest my enemy say, "I have prevailed over him," lest my foes rejoice because I am shaken. 5 But I have trusted in your steadfast love; my heart shall rejoice in your salvation. 6 I will sing to the LORD, because he has dealt bountifully with me.

When you look at David's life, you know he suffered the same temptations, failings, feelings and concerns as we do. I noticed that the Psalm is directed to the choirmaster. That tells me this isn't the first or the last time David was crying out to God, at a loss because he wasn't hearing a response. Jesus answered the question, "how long?" in Parables.

(Luke 11:5-10) *5 And he said to them, "Which of you who has a friend will go to him at midnight and say to him, 'Friend, lend me three loaves, 6 for a friend of mine has arrived on a journey, and I have nothing to set before him'; 7 and he will answer from within, 'Do not bother me; the door is now shut, and my children are with me in bed. I cannot get up and give you anything'?*

8 I tell you, though he will not get up and give him anything because he is his friend, yet because of his impudence he will rise and give him whatever he needs. 9 And I tell you, ask, and it will be given to you; seek, and you will find; knock, and it will be opened to you. 10 For everyone who asks receives, and the one who seeks finds, and to the one who knocks it will be opened.

(Luke 18:1-8) *And he told them a parable to the effect that they ought always to pray and not lose heart. 2 He said, "In a certain city there was a judge who neither feared God nor respected man. 3 And there was a widow in that city who kept coming to him and saying, 'Give me justice against my adversary.' 4 For a while he refused, but afterward he said to himself, 'Though I neither fear God nor respect man, 5 yet because this widow keeps bothering me, I will give her justice, so that she will not beat me down by her continual coming.'"*

6 And the Lord said, "Hear what the unrighteous judge says. 7 And will not God give justice to his elect, who cry to him day and night? Will he delay long over them?

And he told them a parable to the effect that they ought always to pray and not lose heart. 2 He said, 8 I tell you, he will give justice to them speedily. Nevertheless, when the Son of Man comes, will he find faith on earth?"

An important lesson is learned from these teaching Parables. Don't. Give. Up. I've known parents who have prayed for 17 years and more for their children to be saved, business persons who have prayed for decades to have a successful company, and evangelists who have prayed for a life time to see a harvest of souls.

Is God not listening? God hears every prayer we pray, He sees and feels every tear we cry. When we don't see our prayers being answered right NOW, we should trust that God works everything for our good; according to HIS purpose and plan.

(Romans 8:28) *We know that in everything God works for good with those who love him, who are called according to his purpose.* Some Psychologists may see this attitude as "sour grapes." However, according to the scripture, it's the sovereignty of God.

When Joseph wearing his coat of many colors was thrown into the pit by his brothers, he had no idea that what seemed to be evil would be used for great good in the unfolding of God's perfect will.

John Wesley was a great Methodist preacher (June 1703-March 1791), who encountered many times of refusal and denial in his early years of ministry. This is an excerpt from his diary.

+　　Sunday, May 5, A.M. Preached in St. Annes, asked not to come back

+　　Sunday, May 5, P.M. Preached at St. Johns, Deacons said, "get out and stay out!"

+　　Sunday, May 12, A.M. Preached at St. Judes, Can't go back there either

+   Sunday, May 19, P.M. Preached at St. (?) Deacons called special meeting, said I was not to return.

+   Sunday, May 26, A.M. Preached on the street. Kicked off the street

+   Sunday, June 2, A.M. Preached at the edge of town. Kicked off the highway

+   Sunday, June 2, P.M. Preached in a pasture. Ten THOUSAND came.

Friends, continuing effort in a Spirit led direction through prayer, in time, reaps great rewards. (Galatians 6:9) *And let us not grow weary of doing good, for in due season we will reap, if we do not give up.*

The scripture says that whatever we ask in Jesus' name, we receive. (John 14:12-13) *"Truly, truly, I say to you, whoever believes in me will also do the works that I do; and greater works than these will he do, because I am going to the Father. 13 Whatever you ask in my name, this I will do, that the Father may be glorified in the Son.*

Make note this scripture is more like a power of attorney, *"will also do the work that I do,"* than the secret password to tap into endless goodies. It does not mean we get our request immediately. Nor does it mean we can use the name of our Lord to have whatever we want or get out of circumstances we've gotten ourselves into through disobedience.

We often have to live with the circumstances our careless behavior created, but God will, in time, make use of our folly when we commit our hearts to Him. No matter how big our

mistakes have been or how noble our cause is; God is both faithful and sovereign.

When we acknowledge God's presence and His sovereignty, we realize present circumstances are part of a greater plan. Pray without ceasing. Pray with a humble heart, a life that is committed to God is well lived.

(Proverbs 16:9) *The heart of man plans his way, but the LORD establishes his steps.*

I want to encourage you to live strong for Christ. Life is a battle; God has given us the tools we need to live in righteousness, faith and power. Put your armor on, study God's Word, have an ongoing conversation with God and having done all, stand.

Chapter 12

What Is the Destiny of Satan?

We have spent a LOT of pages in this study telling how Satan plans and attacks God's people. I know there are many questions we've left unanswered; perhaps some questions that still need to be asked. This last chapter will try to address some of those questions.

Probably some wonder why we'd even want to "study" Satan, to start with. Isn't it enough to know he's our enemy and his main goal is to ruin our relationship with God and each other? Why would we need any more information other than how to recognize him and instructions to avoid his plans of failure for our lives?

One answer is, because the devil is one of the main characters in the Bible from Genesis to Revelation. Sun Tzu, a philosopher who wrote "The Art of War," more than two thousand years ago summed up why we should know our enemy, "If you know the enemy and know yourself, you need not fear the result of a hundred battles. If you know yourself but not the enemy, for every victory gained you will also suffer a defeat. If you know neither the enemy nor yourself, you will succumb in every battle."

59 times throughout the Bible, the term, "Satan," is used. The Hebrew Scriptures mentions "Satan" 27 times, ten times without the word, "the." (The Satan) Satan is the name given the devil, but the word, Satan, means, "resistor or adversary." In the scriptures, the term, "Satan," is often used to define a human enemy being used as an adversary for evil purposes. Actually, the personage of Satan is mentioned many times, but with different descriptions.

He is also called, The Evil One, the Tempter, the snake, Father of lies, and many more descriptors. Theology commonly speaks of the Devil as the originator and personification of evil. The Devil, Satan, is God's enemy.

The question must be asked, how did Satan become God's enemy? He rebelled against God's authority. There is no scripture that explicitly speaks of the rebellion i.e., "Today Lucifer rebelled and took a third of the angels with him so God cast him out of the heavens."

There are many scriptures that allude to the rebellion of the angel, Lucifer, and how he rebelled taking a third of the angels with him. These two are examples, I'll not quote all the evidences, but, it does make an interesting study.

(Isaiah 14:12-15) *"How you are fallen from heaven, O Lucifer, son of the morning! How you are cut down to the ground, You who weakened the nations! For you have said in your heart: 'I will ascend into heaven, I will exalt my throne above the stars of God; I will also sit on the mount of the congregation On the farthest sides of the north; I will ascend above the heights of the clouds, I will be like the Most High.' Yet you shall be brought down to Sheol, To the lowest depths of the Pit.*

(Revelation 12:4a) *And his tail swept away a third of the stars of heaven and threw them to the earth.*

Doctrine pieces together those defining scriptures and accepts it as evidence of rebellion and expulsion. There is a theological "rule" called the "rule of recurrence," that says when any incident is stated at least three times, it happened. Mention of the heavenly rebellion fulfills that rule.

God is omnipresent, omniscient; He is never, NEVER, surprised. Isaiah 46:9-10 *"-remember the former things of old; for I am God, and there is no other; I am God, and there is none like me, declaring the end from the beginning and from ancient times things not yet done, saying, 'My counsel shall stand, and I will accomplish all my purpose,-'*

God did not create the Devil; He created the angel that would BECOME the Devil. God did not make Lucifer rebel, but He knew that he would. Just like God did not make Judas rebel; He knew that he would. God never tempts us nor does He set us up to fail. (James 1:13) *"When tempted, no one should say, "God is tempting me." For God cannot be tempted by evil, nor does he tempt anyone-"*

However, He knows how "hearts" are (Jeremiah 17:9) *The heart is deceitful above all things, and desperately sick; who can understand it?* ---and obviously, He knew the heart of the angels—as well as mankind, made in His own image.

Not only does He know the rebellion that will happen, He uses that rebellion in the fulfillment of His perfect plan. Many persons in the Bible were taken by evil but their rebellion, once repented, led to God's plan. God is omnipotent and omnipresent. He gives us direction but lets us choose the path we take. When we choose to walk away, His plans for our life do not change. We are free to make our own choices.

When we return to God, the original plan has not changed, but we have. God is faithful to take our brokenness and mold it to fit His sovereign will; that we love Him with all of our heart and do works that will bring Him honor.

There are studies written on the doctrine of rebellion and evil. That is not the purpose of this study, so let's return to our original purpose.

Even though a Christian's attention should be fully devoted to the study of Christ as our life example, we need to be aware of who Satan is and what his goal is. When we study God, (theology always amuses me, "the study of God." That is like a model T studying Henry Ford.) we must also study what is the full extent of His plan for mankind. God's "BIG" plan includes the devil.

In one sense, Satan's judgement began the moment he said, *"I will ascend above the heights of the clouds; I will make myself like the Most High."* (Isaiah 14:14) The full judgement will be seen in three parts, a past judgement, a present judgement and a future judgement.

A good reference point would be in the complexity of thunder and lightning. "Thunder and lightning happen at the same time, but the light travels faster than sound, so the lightning flash reaches your eyes before the sound reaches your ears." (Kidcyber.com) Though both happen at the same time, we have separate experiences, first lightning, then thunder.

So happens the judgement of Satan, the lightning verdict of guilty came from the throne of God. At that point, the war was over; yet the thundering crash of judgement is not yet experienced. Have no doubt, the judgement is coming and will continue throughout eternity.

The "ruler of this world," (2 Corinthians 4:4) *"In their case the god of this world has blinded the minds of the unbelievers, to keep them from seeing the light of the gospel of the glory of Christ, who is the image of God"* the "Prince of the power of the air," (Ephesians 2:1-2) *"And you were dead in the trespasses and sins in which you once walked, following the course of this world, following the prince of the power of the air, the spirit that is now at work in the sons of disobedience"*— will finally receive his just punishment.

Chapter 13
The Three Judgments of Satan

The first judgement was the judgement of positon; Lucifer lost his position in heaven.

(Ezekiel 28:16-17) *In the abundance of your trade you were filled with violence in your midst, and you sinned; so I cast you as a profane thing from the mountain of God, and I destroyed you O guardian cherub, from the midst of the stones of fire.*
Your heart was proud because of your beauty; you corrupted your wisdom for the sake of your splendor. I cast you to the ground; I exposed you before kings, to feast their eyes on you.

His rebellion took one third of the angels with him, *"--and his tail swept away a third of the stars of heaven and threw them to earth."* (Rev. 12:4)

The scriptures, though they don't say so directly, elude that Satan fell before the creation. (Job 38:4-7 particular attention to verse 7) *"Where were you when I laid the foundation of the earth? Tell me, if you have understanding. Who determined its measurements, surely you know! Or who stretched the line upon it. On what were its bases sunk, or who laid its cornerstone,*

7 when the morning stars sang together and all the sons of God shouted for joy?

Obviously, the "sons of God" were the angels; apparently, by the time Satan appeared as a snake in the Garden of Eden, he had fallen out of favor.

While Satan lost his position, it is clear he retained his accountability to God; he still made an occasional appearance before the creator of the Universe.

(Job 1:6-7) *Now there was a day when the sons of God came to present themselves before the LORD, and Satan also came among them. The LORD said to Satan, "From where have you come?" Satan answered the LORD and said, "From going to and fro on the earth, and from walking up and down on it."*

In Luke 22:31 *Jesus said to Simon Peter, "Simon, Simon, behold, Satan demanded to have you that he might sift you like wheat-"*

In Revelation 12:10 John said, "*And I heard a loud voice in heaven, saying, "Now the salvation and the power and the kingdom of our God and the authority of his Christ have come, for the accuser of our brothers has been thrown down, who accuses them day and night before our God."*

Even though Satan was no longer *"--- the anointed cherub that covers; and I have set you so: you were on the holy mountain of God; you have walked up and down in the middle of the stones of fire."* (Ezekiel 28:14) Satan still retained some audience with God; ultimately to fulfill the greater plan of the Almighty.

It is thought that scripture uses the glory of the most excellent ancient state of Tyre, as a comparison to the cherubim which covered the Ark, as a personification of the Devil's former position. The judgment had just started and was far from complete. That was the judgement of position, there followed a judgement of power.

One of my son's favorite movies and action hero is, "Iron Man." Early in the movie, terrorists captured the main character and confined him in a cave. His captor eloquently delivered a historic review of weapons throughout time. The message was "the terrorist who has the biggest weapons, wins."

Think of Satan as the quintessential terrorist and his minions the ultimate terrorist organization. In the Garden of Eden, Satan discovered a powerful weapon that he thought could ruin the plan of God, his archenemy.

What was that weapon? Death, in its fullest sense, physical, spiritual and eternal death is the Devil's ultimate weapon. Satan knew that the holiness of God would require Him to punish sin because, *"—the wages of sin is death--."* (Romans 6:23)

Satan knew humanity had been created for the pleasure of fellowship, even giving man an occupation. (Genesis 1:26) *Then God said, "Let us make man in our image, after our likeness; and let them have dominion over the fish of the sea, and over the birds of the air, and over the cattle, and over all the earth, and over every creeping thing that creeps upon the earth."*

God had warned Adam and Eve about eating the fruit of a specific tree in the Garden. On the surface, it seems that Satan's temptation was simply to cause God's companions to disobey and eat the fruit. However, there is a much deeper sin involved in the scenario. Look closely.

(Genesis 3:1-4*) Now the serpent was more crafty than any other beast of the field that the LORD God had made.*

He said to the woman, "Did God actually say, 'You shall not eat of any tree in the garden'?" And the woman said to the serpent, "We may eat of the fruit of the trees in the garden, but God said, 'You shall not eat of the fruit of the tree that is in the midst of the garden, neither shall you touch it, lest you die.'" But the serpent said to the woman, "You will not surely die."

Do you see the really BIG sin in that scripture? Satan didn't simply tempt Adam and Eve to eat the forbidden fruit; he caused them to question God's sovereignty. "Did God REALLY say that? Do you really believe you will die from eating—fruit? You won't die—."

The exact same type of temptation was given to Jesus when he was being tempted in the wilderness. The scripture is a bit lengthy, but all of it is important to understanding how your enemy works to deceive and discourage you.

Satan wants to put to death your emotional, spiritual, physical and eternal---life. The Devil's tool he used to tempt Jesus was still the same as it was in Eden and, is still the same tool he uses on us today.

(Luke 4:1-13) *And Jesus, full of the Holy Spirit, returned from the Jordan, and was led by the Spirit 2 for forty days in the wilderness, tempted by the devil. And he ate nothing in those days; and when they were ended, he was hungry.*

3 The devil said to him, "If you are the Son of God, command this stone to become bread." 4 And Jesus answered him, "It is written, 'Man shall not live by bread alone.'"

5 And the devil took him up, and showed him all the kingdoms of the world in a moment of time, 6 and said to him, "To you I will give all this authority and their glory; for it has been delivered to me, and I give it to whom I will. 7 If you, then, will worship me, it shall all be yours." 8 And Jesus answered him, "It is written, 'You shall worship the Lord your God, and him only shall you serve.'"

9 And he took him to Jerusalem, and set him on the pinnacle of the temple, and said to him, "If you are the Son of God, throw yourself down from here; 10 for it is written,'He will give his angels charge of you, to guard you,'11 and 'On their hands they will bear you up, lest you strike your foot against a stone.'"

12 And Jesus answered him, "It is said, 'You shall not tempt the Lord your God.'" 13 And when the devil had ended every temptation, he departed from him until an opportune time.

Can you see it? Satan used the exact same tactic to try to defeat Jesus, the Son of God, fully God yet fully man, to sin. What was the sin; to deny the sovereignty of God. Notice how each time the Devil tried to tempt Jesus, the response was—"it is written," or, "GOD said."

How different our lives would be if every time Satan tempts us with fear, anger, rebellion, going our own way, discouragement, the list goes on—we responded, in full knowledge of God's sovereignty of our lives, with, "GOD says."
Because of Christ's death at Calvary, we no longer need to fear death. God is sovereign over all death, even eternal death. Even though our physical bodies are subject to pain and death; *"-- do not fear those who kill the body but cannot kill the soul. Rather fear him who can destroy both soul and body in hell."* (Matthew 10:28)

Satan's goal is to separate us from God not just now, but for eternity. Statistically, three people die every second, 260,000 die every day, 95 million people die every year. If the Devil had his way, every person that God created for fellowship with Himself, will be separated from Him for eternity. Satan's plan is to rob God's people of being in God's presence by the eternal separation of death. *"—the wages of sin is death."*

So, how has God made Satan powerless over his ultimate weapon, death? (Hebrews 2:14) *Since therefore the children share in flesh and blood, <u>he himself likewise partook of the same things, that through death he might destroy the one who has the power of death, that is, the devil,</u> 15 and deliver all those who through fear of death were subject to lifelong slavery. 16 For surely it is not angels that he helps, but he helps the offspring of Abraham.* (Emphasis on underline, mine)

Satan's power position to separate us from our loving God was terminated at Calvary. After Adam sinned, God informed Satan that his victory was minor: (Galatians 3:14-15*) 14 The LORD God said to the serpent, "Because you have done this, cursed are you above all livestock and above all beasts of the field; on your belly you shall go, and dust you shall eat all the days of your life. 15 I will put enmity between you and the woman, and between your offspring and her offspring; he shall bruise your head, and you shall bruise his heel."*

The biggest power grab was planned at Calvary; Satan thought he had it all wrapped up. By crucifying Jesus, the plan of death would be solidified. Done, finished, the plan of God, all for naught.

Satan didn't delegate the grand finale to a subservient demon; he personally entered Judas Iscariot at the last meal Jesus shared with His disciples, the Passover feast. (John 13:27) *Then after he had taken the morsel, Satan entered into him. Jesus said to him, "What you are going to do, do quickly."*

I'm not going to print the entire thirteenth chapter of the Gospel of John here, but I encourage you to read the whole chapter. You will see the Devil's scheme to make his final move the best ever. Satan planned to end it all with the crucifixion, then He would be more powerful than God. As you read the chapter, note that Jesus knew every plan Satan had made, the betrayal and death was not a surprise. Jesus even spoke of what was ahead to His Disciples, but they couldn't understand.

Satan didn't realize that through Jesus' death on Calvary, the greatest enemy of all, death, would be defeated. Can you imagine the glee of Satan as the drama of the Crucifixion played out? The Devil emptied all his barrels, threw every weapon he had on the Son of God.

Before we go on to the final victory over death, sin and the grave, I know there is a question you want to ask. Did Judas HAVE to betray Christ? Was he given no other choice, was he doomed from his birth to play this part of betrayal?

God did not create Judas to betray Jesus, but God knew that he would. At any point, Judas could have repented and been a true follower; he was human and made choices just like we do. Remember, Judas sought out and bargained with those who wanted to kill Jesus; the betrayal was planned in the rebellion of his own heart. His own rebellion opened the door and Satan entered into him.

(Luke 22:1-7) *Now the Feast of Unleavened Bread drew near, which is called the Passover. 2 And the chief priests and the scribes were seeking how to put him to death, for they feared the people.*

3 Then Satan entered into Judas called Iscariot, who was of the number of the twelve. 4 He went away and conferred with the chief priests and officers how he might betray him to them. 5 And they were glad, and agreed to give him money. 6 So he consented and sought an opportunity to betray him to them in the absence of a crowd.

Judas was given a free will, just like us, to do whatever we choose to do. At any point, Judas could have turned, confessed and repented. But, he didn't. Judas chose not to be a follower; he hardened his own heart, and consequently, gave himself over to Satan. How can we know that Judas had hardened his heart beforehand?

Before the Passover meal where Judas was taken by Satan, he was at another dinner, at the home of Lazarus. Mary, Lazarus sister, washed Jesus' feet with costly perfume as an act of love. (John 12:4-6) *4 But Judas Iscariot, one of his disciples (he who was about to betray him), said, 5 "Why was this ointment not sold for three hundred denarii and given to the poor?" 6 He said this, not because he cared about the poor, but because he was a thief, and having charge of the moneybag he used to help himself to what was put into it.*

Still today, Satan doesn't just take over; we open the door and give him a foothold. There are eternal consequences to our everyday choices; we either accept Christ or we allow our heart to become hardened, giving Satan a foothold.

Now, let's go back to the victory of Calvary, unfolding before us. The Disciples didn't know what the crucifixion was about. The people had thought that Jesus had come to set up His heavenly kingdom on earth.

(Luke 19:11) *As they heard these things, he proceeded to tell a parable, because he was near to Jerusalem, and because they supposed that the kingdom of God was to appear immediately.*

(Matthew 20:20-21) *Then the mother of the sons of Zebedee came up to him with her sons, and kneeling before him she asked him for something. And he said to her, "What do you want?" She said to him, "Say that these two sons of mine are to sit, one at your right hand and one at your left, in your kingdom."*

(Luke 17: 20-21) *Being asked by the Pharisees when the kingdom of God would come, he answered them, "The kingdom of God is not coming in ways that can be observed, 21 nor will they say, 'Look, here it is!' or 'There!' for behold, the kingdom of God is in the midst of you."*

Even after Jesus had died and been resurrected, He showed himself to the Disciples as they were walking along the road together and still they thought the Kingdom of God was going to be set up on earth at that moment. (Acts 1:6) *So when they had come together, they asked him, "Lord, will you at this time restore the kingdom to Israel?"*

Back to the cross at Calvary, the Crucifixion is happening. The Disciples and Jesus' mother and brothers were in shock; this was not how it was supposed to end. Remember, they thought Jesus was going to set up His Kingdom on earth right away--. Instead, He was being brutally murdered, right before their eyes.

Only Jesus and God, the Father, knew what was going on. Savagely beaten, bearing in His body the full payment for our sickness and sins, Jesus hung between heaven and earth, in agony. But wait, it was not the brutal crucifixion that paid for our sins! In those times, many were crucified; it was no special punishment thought up just for the Christ.

The wages of sin is—death. Spiritual death is the eternal separation from God, who created us for companionship. To be thrown into outer darkness, with no comfort, no presence, only pain and emptiness, the total absence of God.

When Jesus took on the sins of the world, all the sins, throughout time dropped on Him. Murder, rebellion, theft, abuse, anger, bitterness---greed--selfishness---ALL sin, big and small was placed on Jesus.

God is Holy; He can't be where sin is. Light can't exist with darkness. (2 Corinthians 6:14) *Do not be unequally yoked with unbelievers. For what partnership has righteousness with lawlessness? Or what fellowship has light with darkness?* (underlining mine)

As the crushing weight of the sins of all mankind dropped on Jesus, God turned away. At that moment, Jesus felt the full blow of separation from God. The anguished cry from the cross, *"My God! My God, why have you forsaken me?"* He cried out, *"IT IS FINISHED!"* (John 19:30a)

When he had received the drink, fulfilling prophesy of the crucifixion, (Psalms 69:21) *They gave me poison for food, and for my thirst they gave me sour wine to drink.* Jesus cried out, "It is finished."

(Matthew 27:46-50) *And about the ninth hour Jesus cried with a loud voice, "Eli, Eli, la'ma sabach-tha'ni?" that is, "My God, my God, why hast thou forsaken me?" And some of the bystanders hearing it said, "This man is calling Eli'jah." And one of them at once ran and took a sponge, filled it with vinegar, and put it on a reed, and gave it to him to drink. But the others said, "Wait, let us see whether Eli'jah will come to save him." And Jesus cried again with a loud voice and yielded up his spirit.*

The sin debt that had separated us from God, was paid in full.

The moment of completion, the full payment for sin, shook the universe. The veil in the temple that separated individuals from the Holy altar of God was torn in half. In that one moment, we were given access to come into God's presence, face to face! The earth quaked, the dead came up from the ground and walked the streets.

(Matthew 27:51) *And behold, the curtain of the temple was torn in two, from top to bottom; and the earth shook, and the rocks were split; the tombs also were opened, and many bodies of the saints who had fallen asleep were raised, and coming out of the tombs after his resurrection they went into the holy city and appeared to many.*

When the sins of all humanity fell on the Christ, our sin debt was paid in full throughout all eternity.
(Colossians 2:14-15) *--by canceling the record of debt that stood against us with its legal demands. This he set aside, nailing it to the cross. He disarmed the rulers and authorities and put them to open shame, by triumphing over them in him.*

Satan was removed from his position by the decree of God. Then, the Devil lost all of his power by the death and resurrection of Jesus. However, there is one other judgement still to come. The Judgement of Presence, Satan will be thrown into the pit with all his demons and those who chose to follow evil rather than God. Hell was not created for people; we have to CHOOSE to go there.

(Matthew 25:41) *"Then he will say to those on his left, 'Depart from me, you accursed, into the eternal fire that has been prepared for the devil and his angels!"*

When Christ returns, Revelation 20 says that Satan will be bound in the Pit for a thousand years, during the Millennial Reign of Christ.

(Revelation 20:1-3) *Then I saw an angel coming down from heaven, holding in his hand the key to the bottomless pit and a great chain. 2 And he seized the dragon, that ancient serpent, who is the devil and Satan, and bound him for a thousand years,*

3 and threw him into the pit, and shut it and sealed it over him, so that he might not deceive the nations any longer, until the thousand years were ended. After that he must be released for a little while.

During this time, Jesus Christ will literally and physically make His throne on Earth, ruling this planet. For the first time since the fall of man, peace will prevail. Then, John the Revelator tells us, (Revelation 20:3) *He threw him into the Abyss, and locked and sealed it over him, to keep him from deceiving the nations anymore until the thousand years were ended. After that, he must be set free for a short time.*

(Revelation 20: 7-10) *And when the thousand years are ended, Satan will be released from his prison 8 and will come out to deceive the nations that are at the four corners of the earth, Gog and Magog, to gather them for battle; their number is like the sand of the sea.*

9 And they marched up over the broad plain of the earth and surrounded the camp of the saints and the beloved city, but fire came down from heaven and consumed them, 10 and the devil who had deceived them was thrown into the lake of fire and sulfur where the beast and the false prophet were, and they will be tormented day and night forever and ever.

Think of it, no more demonic temptations, no more strongholds, accusations, torments, sicknesses, fear, failures or defeats. The greatest Battle of all time, thousands of years in the waiting for conclusion, will finally be—finished.

Bill and Gloria Gaither sums the moment up in their glorious song, "It Is Finished!"

It Is Finished!

It is finished! The Battle is over!

It is finished! There'll be no more war!

It is finished! The end of the conflict.

It is finished! And Jesus *is* LORD!

(Bill and Gloria Gaither, Gaither Vocal Band, 2000)